AF574279

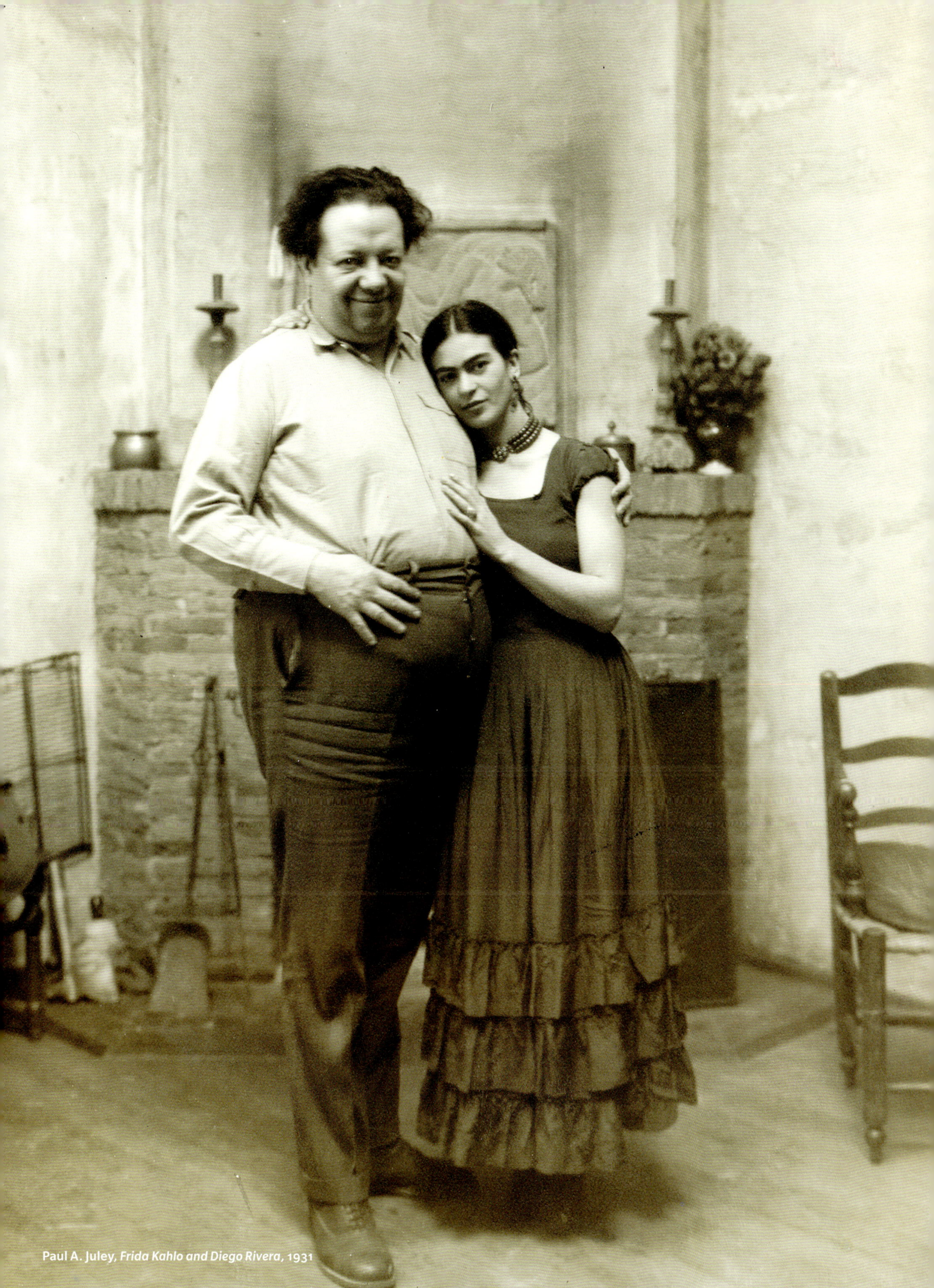

Paul A. Juley, *Frida Kahlo and Diego Rivera*, 1931

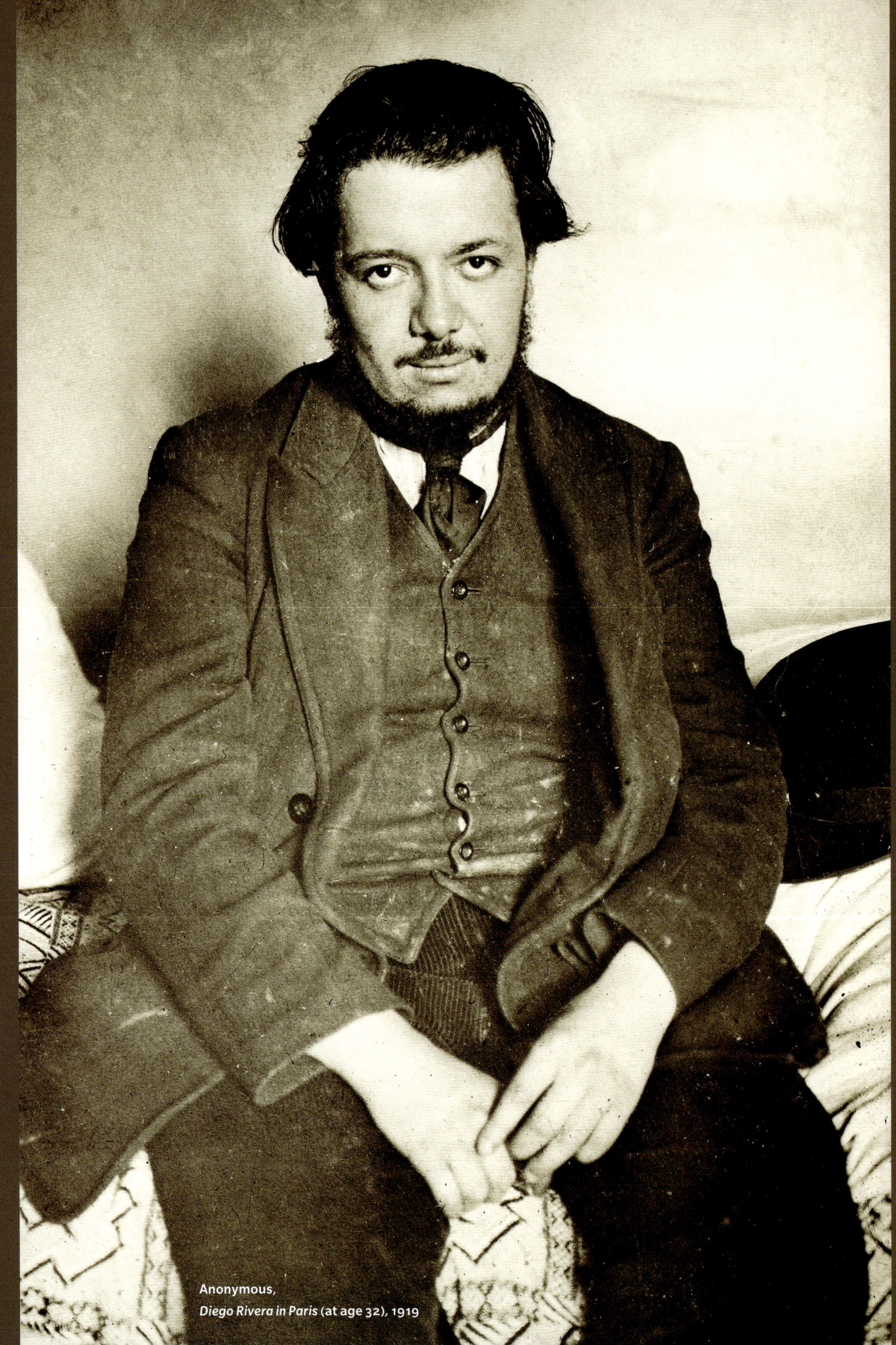

Anonymous,
Diego Rivera in Paris (at age 32), 1919

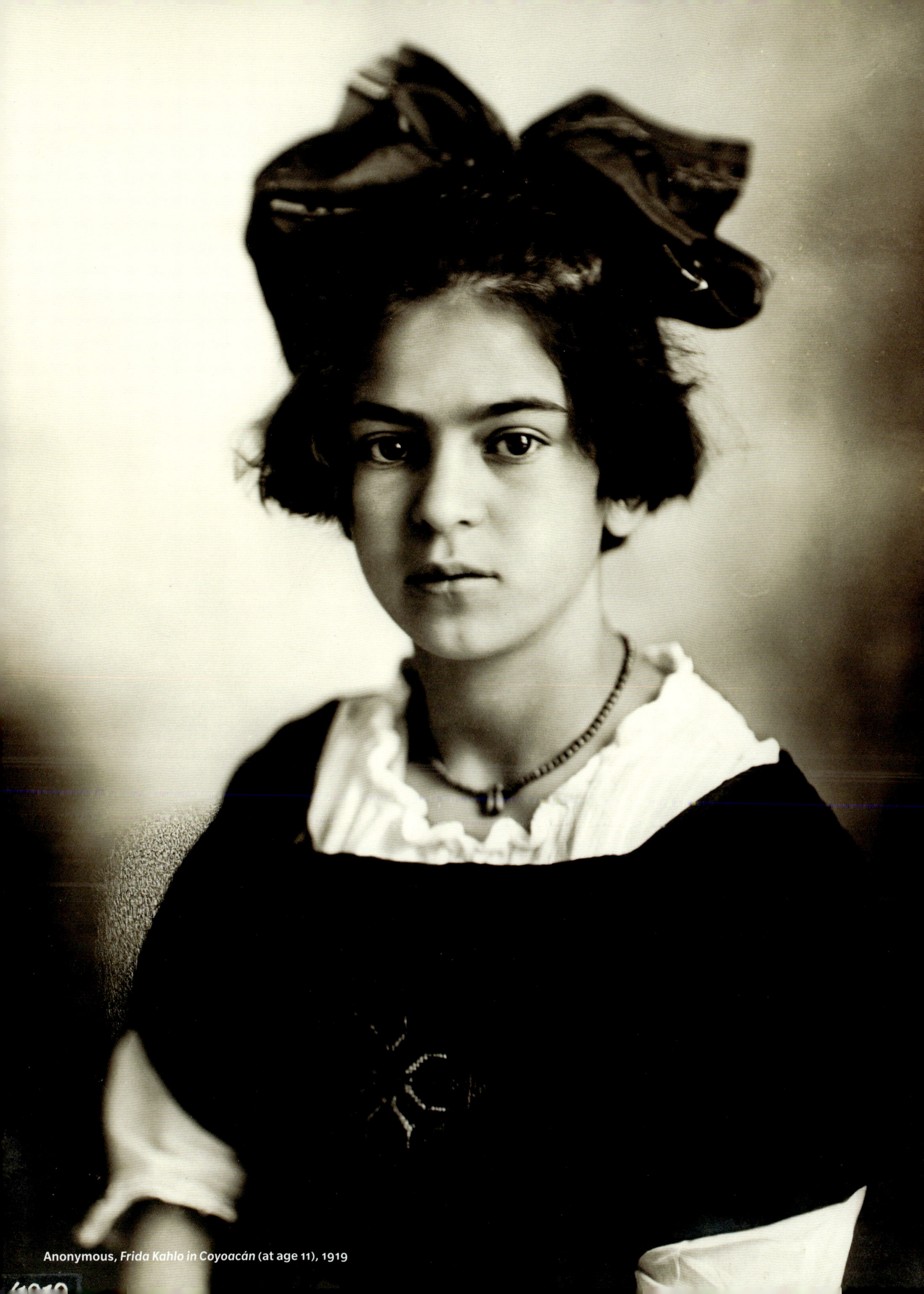

Anonymous, *Frida Kahlo in Coyoacán* (at age 11), 1919

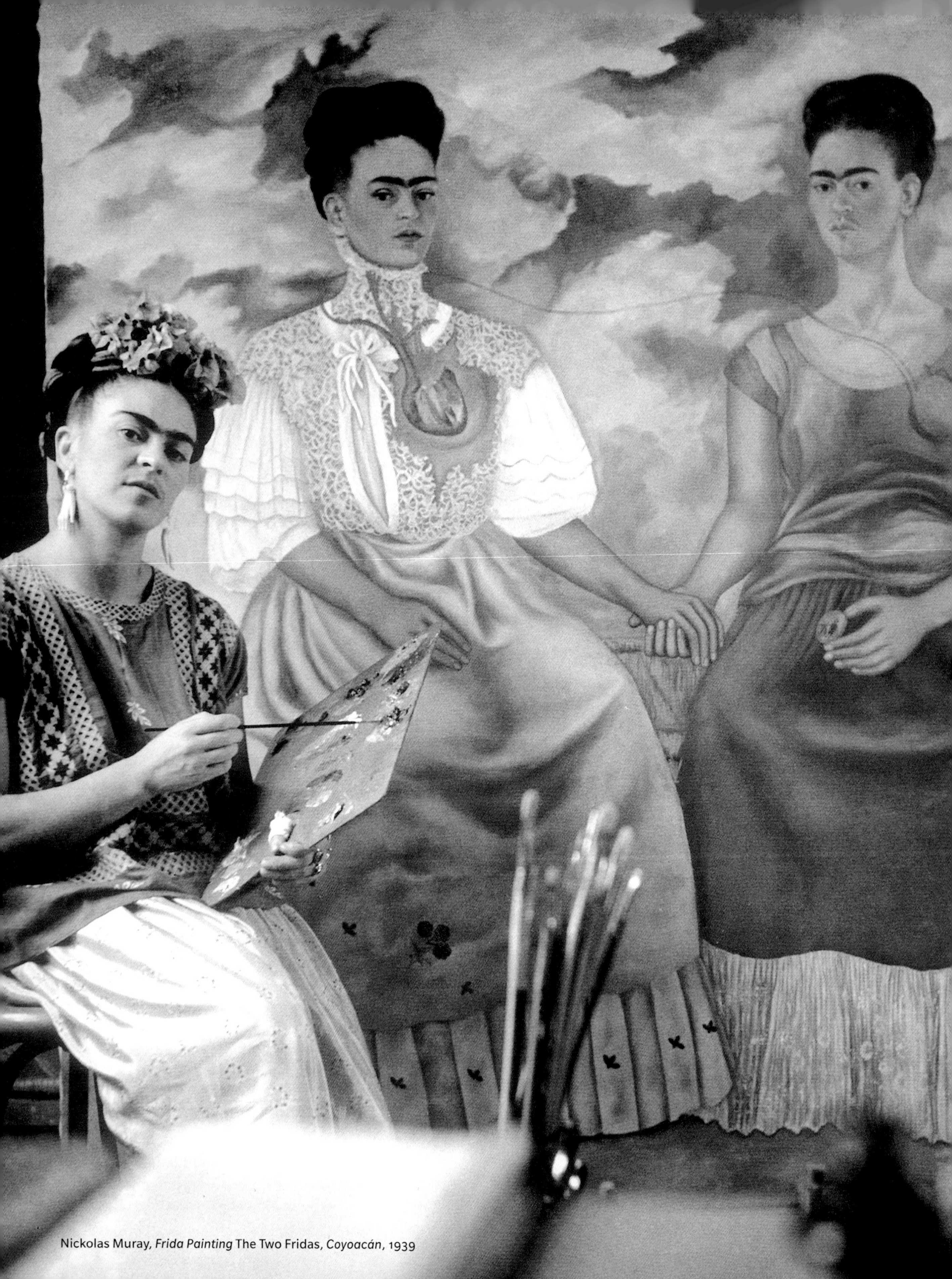

Nickolas Muray, *Frida Painting* The Two Fridas, *Coyoacán*, 1939

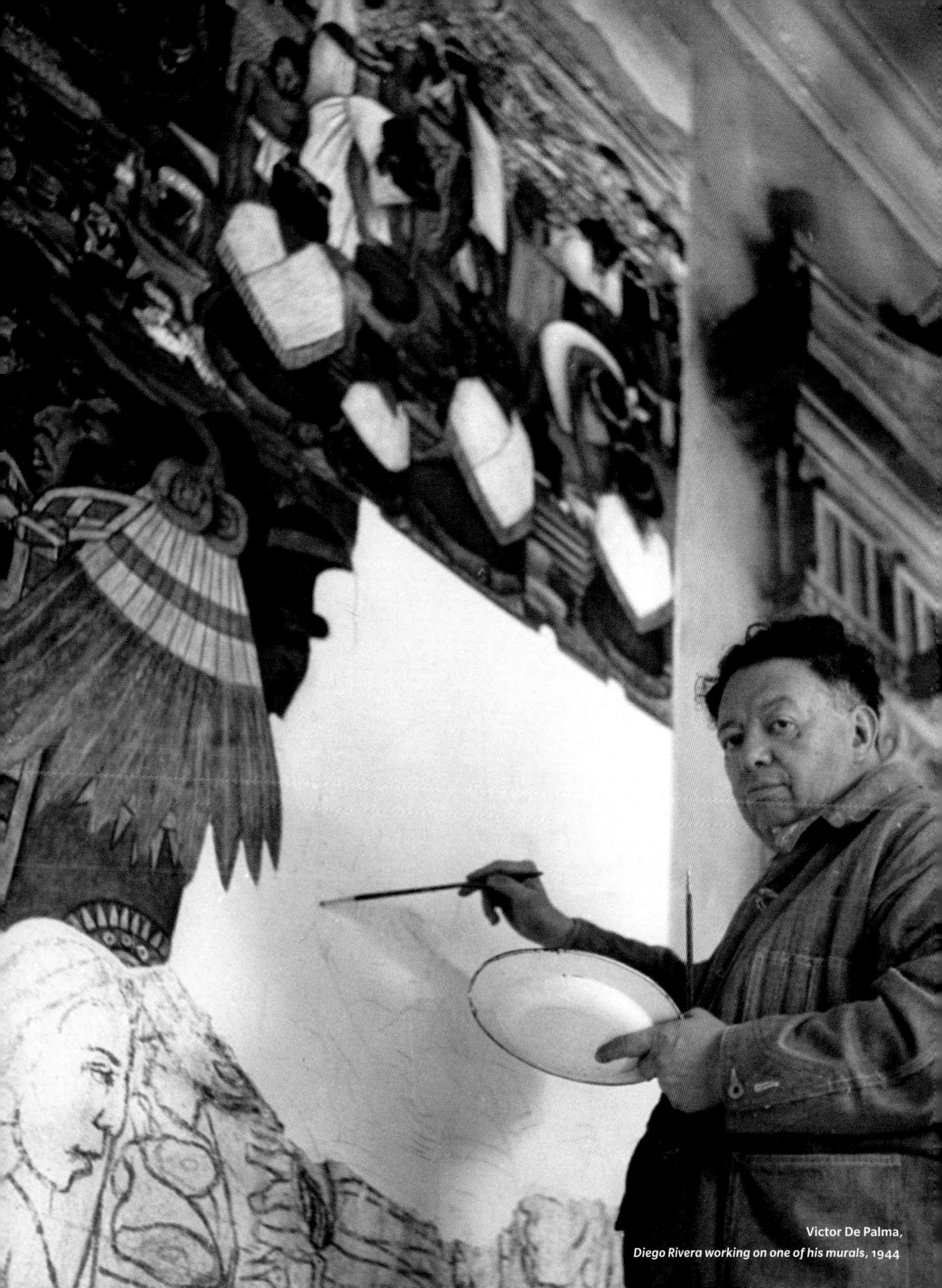

Victor De Palma,
Diego Rivera working on one of his murals, 1944

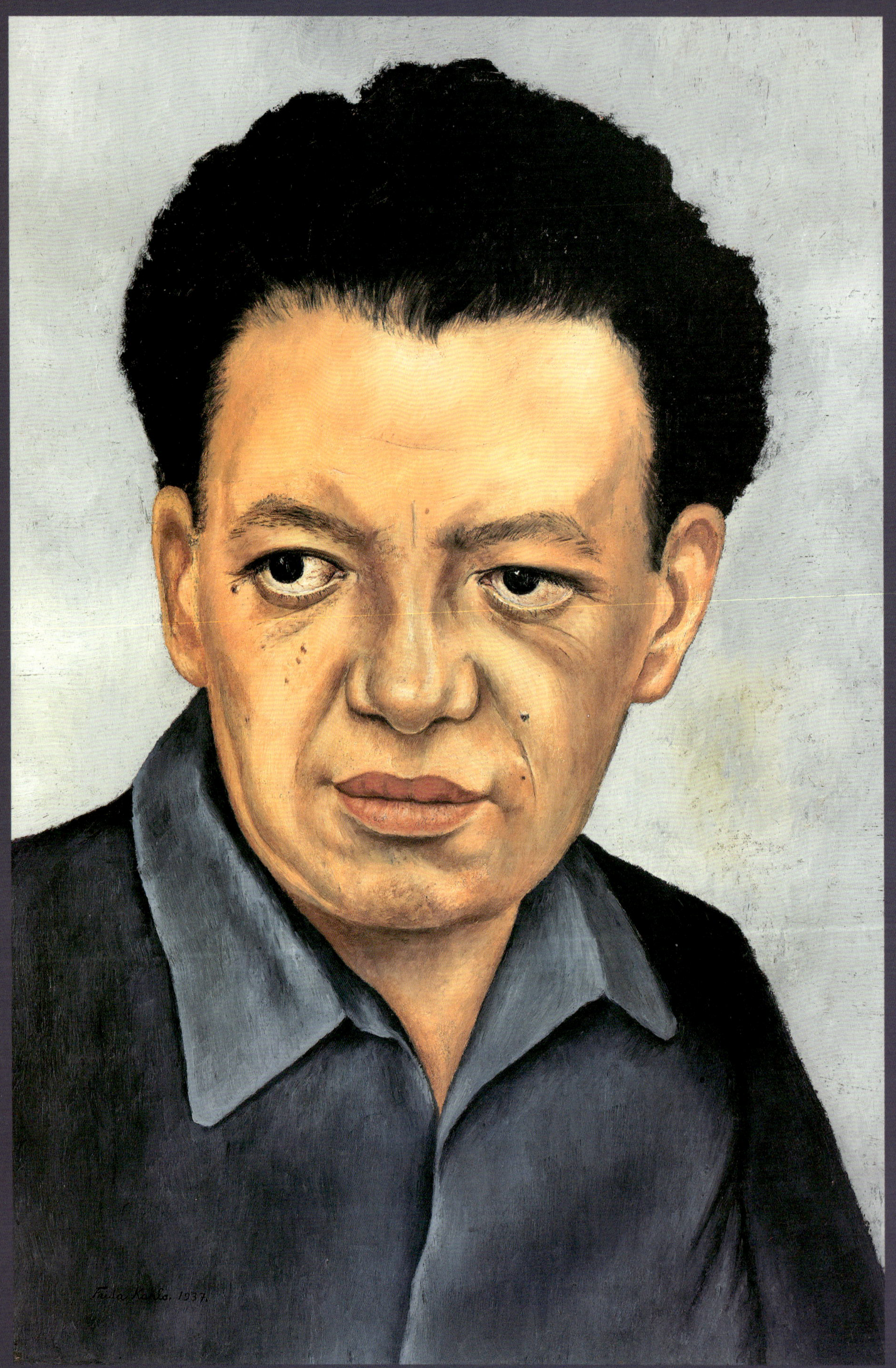

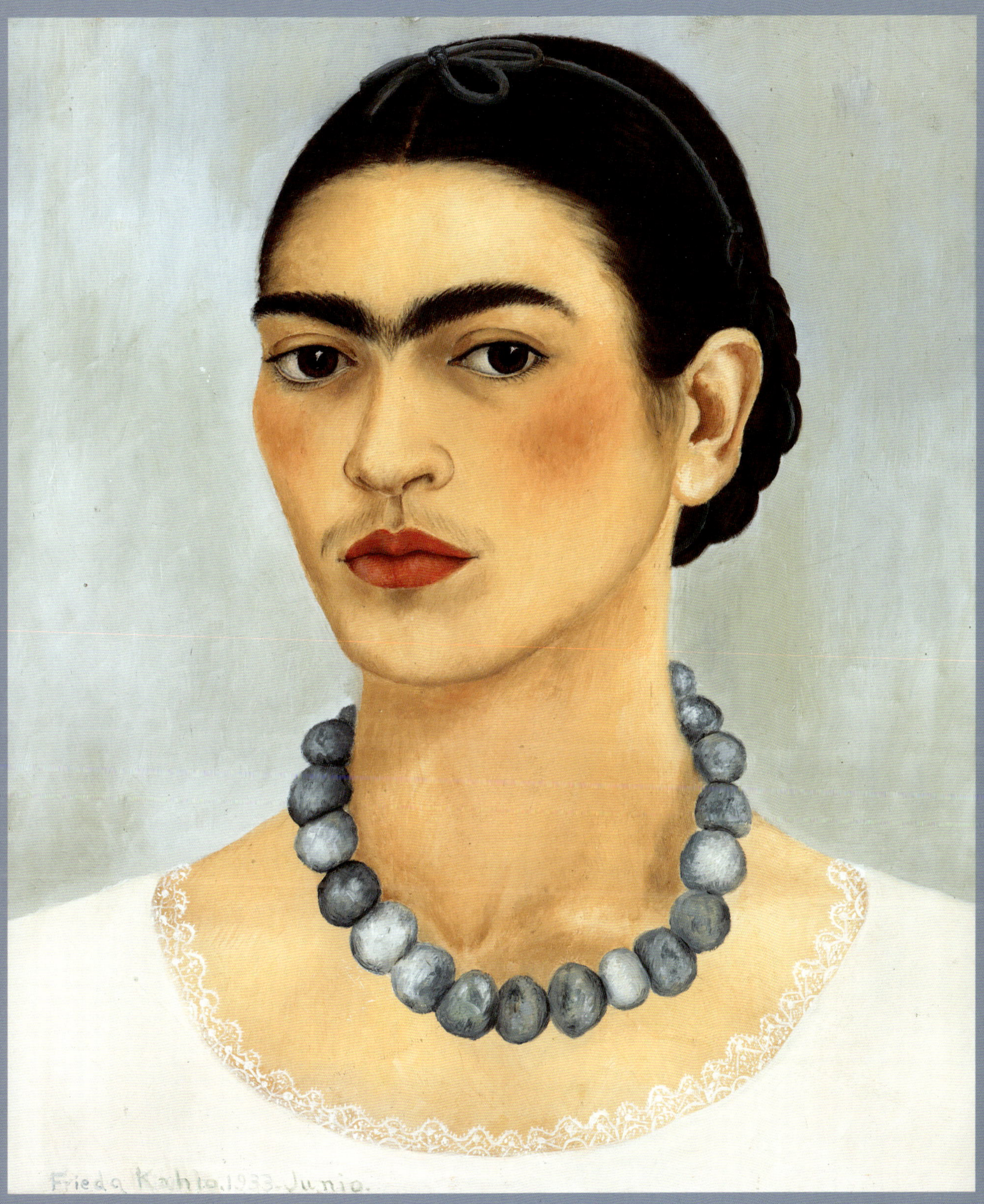

◀ Frida Kahlo *Portrait of Diego Rivera*, 1937

▲ Frida Kahlo *Self-Portrait with Necklace*, 1933

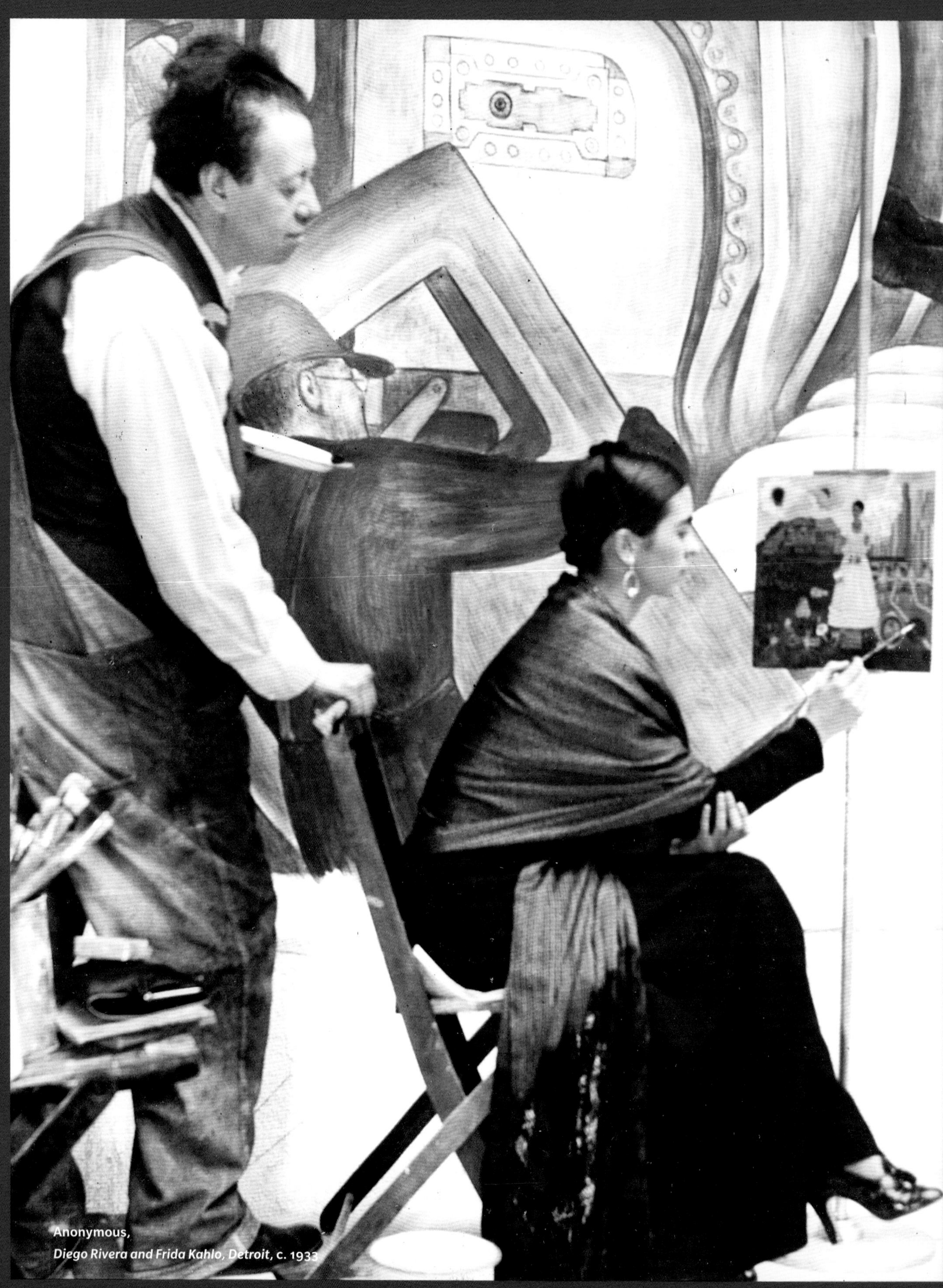

Anonymous,
Diego Rivera and Frida Kahlo, Detroit, c. 1933

FRIDA & DIEGO

PASSION, POLITICS AND PAINTING

EDITED BY DOT TUER AND ELLIOTT KING

Art Gallery of Ontario / High Museum of Art, Atlanta

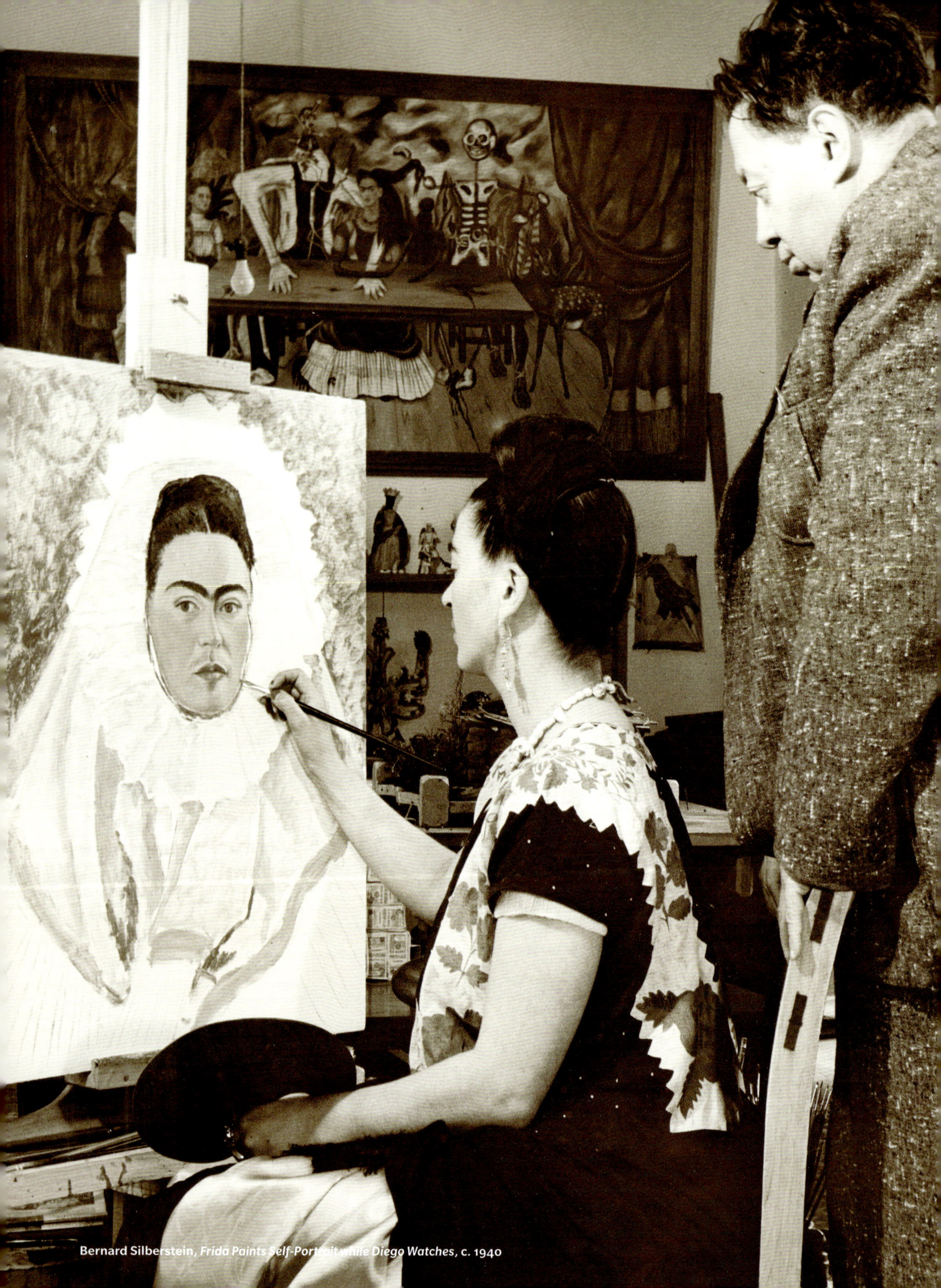

Bernard Silberstein, *Frida Paints Self-Portrait while Diego Watches*, c. 1940

CONTENTS

DIRECTORS' FOREWORD

Few artists are as crystallized in the public imagination as Frida Kahlo and Diego Rivera, yet despite their nearly twenty-five years together as a married couple, their art has rarely been paired in an exhibition. This is largely due to the perception that they worked in very different styles and with separate intentions. Rivera was twenty years older than Kahlo and had achieved international prominence as Mexico's greatest mural painter in the Golden Age of Mexican art, the 1920s, when Kahlo was only a teenager. His monumental wall paintings depict the heroic struggles of Mexican history, drawing on indigenous art styles with an imperative to unite the working class in support of Communist revolution. On the surface, Kahlo's paintings are very different. Where Rivera was grandiose and highly public, Kahlo was intimate, communicating her own profound physical and emotional suffering through small-scale still life paintings and penetrating self-portraits, many of which she gifted privately to close friends. It was not until the 1970s, nearly twenty years after the deaths of both artists, that Kahlo's art attained the respect and acclaim it enjoys today. As individual artists, each has now achieved international stature in the history of modern painting; however, the two remain artistically isolated from one another.

In bringing the works of these two artists together, the exhibition *Frida & Diego: Passion, Politics and Painting* offers a new perspective on Kahlo and Rivera's significance, acknowledging how their paintings reflect the dramatic story of their life together as well as their shared artistic commitment to the political and cultural values of post-revolutionary Mexico. Assembled from three distinguished Mexican private collections—the Museo Dolores Olmedo, Colección Gelman, and Galería Arvil—and combined with works from other international museums and private collections, the exhibition provides an opportunity to view almost one-quarter of Kahlo's entire body of work. It presents her works in direct relation to a range of Rivera's, from his early Cubist period and studies for Mexican murals to his portraits and later landscapes.

The partnership between the Art Gallery of Ontario in Toronto, the High Museum of Art in Atlanta, and the Museo Dolores Olmedo in Mexico City—in association with The Vergel Foundation, The Jacques and Natasha Gelman Collection of Mexican Art, and Galería Arvil—has deepened in preparation for this exhibition. We remain grateful to the following individuals who have continued to work unflaggingly to ensure the project's success: Jan August Hendrickx; Mary-Anne Martin; Rosa María Rodríguez Garza, Manager of Cultural Programs, FEMSA; and Bertha Cea Echenique, Senior Cultural Affairs Specialist, U.S. Embassy in Mexico. We would also like to thank the following individuals and organizations for generously lending artworks to this groundbreaking exhibition: Anonymous donor; Michael Audain and Yoshiko Karasawa; Ann and Harry Malcolmson; Patricia Regan; Albright-Knox Art Gallery, Buffalo; Artemundi Group; Coca-Cola FEMSA; Mimi Levitt; Los Angeles County Museum of Art, California; The Museum of Modern Art, New York; National Gallery of Art, Washington D.C.; Nickolas Muray Photo Archives; Royal Ontario Museum, Toronto; and Throckmorton Fine Arts, Inc., New York.

A collaboration of this magnitude demands significant resources. The High Museum of Art is profoundly grateful for the early support provided by the Forward Arts Foundation, The Sara Giles Moore Foundation, MetLife Foundation, and the Eleanor McDonald Storza Exhibition Endowment Fund. The AGO is eminently grateful for the special support of Gretchen & Donald Ross, and the generous assistance of Scott & Krystyne Griffin and Valerie Greenfield & Hunter Thompson, whose contributions were vital in helping us achieve the level of excellence for which we strive. In addition, the AGO would like to acknowledge the support of the Department of Canadian Heritage through the Canada Travelling Exhibitions Indemnification Program, the Ontario Cultural Attractions Fund, and Celebrate Ontario, all of which played a key role in securing this exhibition.

Most importantly, we would like to extend our sincerest thanks to exhibition curators Dot Tuer and Elliott King, who have made the process a pleasure for both institutions. It is to their credit that the exhibition and publication each turned out to be as exceptional as we had envisioned.

Matthew Teitelbaum
Michael and Sonja Koerner Director, and CEO, Art Gallery of Ontario

Michael E. Shapiro
Nancy and Holcombe T. Green, Jr., Director, High Museum of Art

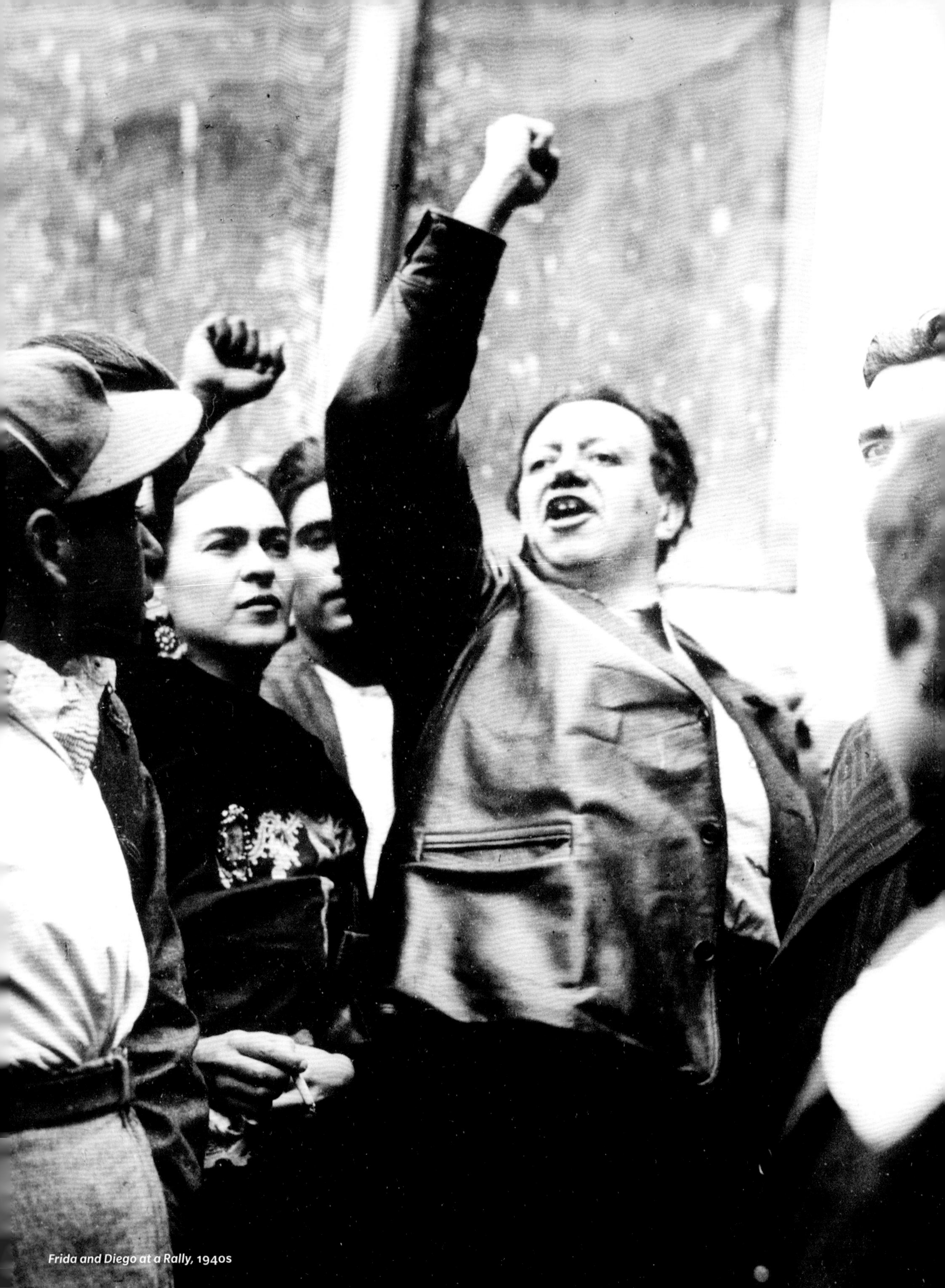

Frida and Diego at a Rally, 1940s

OF PASSION AND PAINTING

THE REVOLUTIONARY POLITICS OF DIEGO RIVERA AND FRIDA KAHLO

When Frida Kahlo married Diego Rivera on August 21, 1929, she was twenty-two years of age and a novice painter; he was twenty years her senior and at the height of his creative powers as a muralist. Between 1923 and 1929, he had completed more than 200 large fresco panels for the Ministry of Education courtyard in Mexico City and the National Agricultural School in Chapingo. In 1931, his solo exhibition at The Museum of Modern Art in New York City consolidated his reputation as a world-renowned artist. During their lifetime together, Rivera's fame as a muralist overshadowed Kahlo's creation of an intimate yet equally significant body of work comprising primarily self-portraits and still lifes. Whereas Rivera was academically trained and prolific—producing hundreds of paintings, watercolours, sketches, and lithographs, as well as covering the walls of Mexico's most important institutions—Kahlo was self-taught and painstakingly measured, completing fewer than 200 small works before her death in 1954 at the age of forty-seven. While her art was embraced by the Surrealist movement in the late 1930s, her first solo exhibition in Mexico did not take place until 1953, and she remained largely unrecognized in the broader context of modern art until the 1970s.

In recent decades, Kahlo's posthumous fame has eclipsed that of Rivera, who died three years after her in 1957. A proliferation of biographies, films, and websites has secured her cult status in popular culture. Numerous exhibitions have enshrined her as one of modernism's most profound women artists, whose self-portraits embody both the physical suffering she endured after a debilitating bus accident and the spiritual anguish caused by Rivera's infidelity and her inability to have children. In contrast, Rivera's reputation as an artist declined with the onset of the Cold War and the rise of Abstract Expressionism. By the 1960s, muralism had become the domain of community activism rather than the avant-garde, and Rivera's affiliation with Communism led to his murals being dismissed as political propaganda and cartoonish as often as they were lauded for their sweeping embrace of history and dense figuration. Despite major retrospectives of his work in Mexico City, London, and Detroit since 1986, Rivera no longer looms larger-than-life in the public imagination as Mexico's greatest muralist accompanied by a much younger and diminutive wife. Instead, Frida is seen as the iconic artist with Diego cast in a minor role as her much older and philandering husband.

In bringing the work of Kahlo and Rivera together, *Frida & Diego: Passion, Politics and Painting* explores the affinities as well as differences that shaped the dynamics of their relationship and distinctive oeuvres. As a couple, the early years of their marriage were emotionally volatile—Diego's compulsive seduction of women and Frida's affairs culminated in a year-long divorce at the end of 1939—while the latter years of their remarriage were subsumed by Frida's declining health. As artists, their shared belief in the revolutionary potential of socialism and the transformative values of *mestizaje* (the mixing of indigenous and European peoples and traditions) sustained their devotion to each other for a quarter century. Rivera's mission was, in his own words, to "reflect the social life of Mexico as I saw it, and through my vision of the truth to show the masses the outline of the future."[1] Kahlo, who famously declared, "I paint my own reality,"[2] captured the complexity of gender and race relations through an autobiographical lens, which affirmed her independence as a woman and her mestiza identity. Together, their story is one in which their passion for painting was inseparable from a politics shaped by two great revolutions of the twentieth century: the Mexican Revolution of 1910 and the Russian Revolution of 1917.

When the Mexican Revolution began in 1910, Rivera was twenty-four years old. Born in 1886 in Guanajuato, he had demonstrated a precocious artistic talent that gained him entrance to the Academy of San Carlos in Mexico City, where he studied art from 1898 to 1905, and secured a scholarship to further his training in Spain in 1907. Kahlo was born the same year that Rivera left for Europe, but gave her birth date as 1910 to coincide with the birth of the revolutionary upheaval in her homeland that led to a decade of armed struggle, the assassination of most of the Revolution's leaders—including Francisco Madero, Emiliano Zapata, and Pancho Villa—and the loss of more than one million lives. In her diary, Kahlo claims that as a small child she witnessed street clashes between opposing revolutionary forces in 1914, relating that her mother sheltered and fed Zapata's soldiers, who had fled their adversaries by leaping into the living room of the Casa Azul (The Blue House), Kahlo's family home in the Mexico City suburb of Coyoacán where she was born and ultimately died.[3] Whether Kahlo actually witnessed factional fighting is doubtful, although Zapata's army did occupy the city in 1914. For Kahlo personally, 1914 was more significant as the year that she contracted polio, which permanently damaged her right leg. And while she and her family suffered economic hardship during the Revolution, they did not experience its carnage. This occurred primarily in the north of Mexico, where battles were waged for control of the country, and in the south, where Zapata's guerrilla *campesinos* (rural workers) fought bitterly for the promise of agrarian reform.

In his autobiography, Rivera similarly touts his revolutionary credentials, claiming that he fought on the front lines with Zapata.[4] In fact, he was absent from Mexico for most of the revolutionary period. After briefly returning home from Spain in 1910, Rivera left for Europe the next year and lived in Paris until 1921. When Zapata was marching on Mexico City in 1914, Rivera was meeting Pablo Picasso in Paris cafés and following the Revolution's course of events through news reports and contact with Mexicans traveling overseas. Towards the end of his lengthy sojourn in Paris, Rivera met David Alfaro Siqueiros, a young painter who had experienced the Revolution's carnage first-hand, and who later became, along with Rivera and José Clemente Orozco, one of the three great Mexican muralists of the post-revolutionary period. During their time spent together in Europe, Siqueiros and Rivera discussed the need for an art that reflected Mexico's social transformation. In 1923, they issued the Manifesto of the Union of Technical Workers, Painters, and Sculptors, which called for a monumental art of the people. Equally important for Rivera's politicization as an artist was his ten-year relationship in Paris with Angela Beloff, whose circle of Russian émigrés influenced Rivera's commitment to Communism born of the Russian Revolution and the seizure of power by Vladimir Lenin's Bolshevik Marxists in October 1917.

As the Mexican Revolution drew to a close in 1920, Rivera was recruited by José Vasconcelos – one of the Revolution's cultural ideologues and Minister of Education from 1921 to 1924 – to participate in his plan to sponsor public murals in order to promote a cultural nationalism forged from popular folk traditions and the fusion of indigenous and Western civilizations. At Vasconcelos's request, Rivera traveled to Italy in 1920 to study Renaissance frescoes, and then visited the Mayan ruins in the southern state of Yucatán after returning to Mexico in 1921. The next year Rivera joined the Communist Party and married Guadalupe Marín, with whom he would have two children. He also began work on his first mural, *Creation*, whose classical references and pyramid of corn were a hint of how he would synthesize European and indigenous artistic influences. It was while Rivera worked on this mural, located in the auditorium of the National Preparatory School where Kahlo was a student, that she first laid eyes on her future husband. It was not until 1928, however, when Rivera returned from a ten-month visit to the Soviet Union and separated from Marín, that he began to court Kahlo, calling on her weekly at her Coyoacán home and painting her as a young revolutionary distributing arms to the people in his fresco on the third floor of the Ministry of Education building.

In the intervening years, their fates could not have been more different. In 1922, Kahlo was admitted to the prestigious National Preparatory School, one of only thirty-five girls out of 2,000 students. Planning to become a doctor, she demonstrated an intelligence as precocious as Rivera's artistic talent, and flouted social conventions, cutting her hair short like a *pelona*, a Mexican version of a flapper. Then, in 1925, her world was irrevocably altered when a trolley sliced through a bus she was riding on, breaking her spinal column, ribs, collarbone, and pelvis as well as crushing her left shoulder, fracturing her right leg, and piercing her abdomen. While Rivera was painting for sixteen-hour stretches at the Ministry of Education, surrounded by admirers who traveled from Europe and North America to watch him at work and train as his assistants, Kahlo's life as an artist began in isolation. She made her first paintings during the months she lay immobilized in bed and spent several years at home convalescing from the accident. Although she made an astonishing recovery, she was left slightly crippled and continued to undergo numerous operations on her damaged spine and right leg in the decades that followed. By 1927, Kahlo was well enough to become involved in radical politics and bohemian art circles. Through her friendship with Tina Modotti, an Italian-American photographer and Rivera's former lover, she joined the Communist Party in 1928.

While Kahlo and Rivera most likely met at one of Modotti's parties, both artists tell another story, one where Kahlo, paintings in hand, went to the Ministry of Education to demand of Rivera that he descend from his scaffold to give her an honest opinion of her work, upon which the great maestro obliged her by pronouncing, "You have talent."[5] The story may have been invented, but Rivera's admiration for Kahlo's creative vision never faltered. In 1938, he wrote to an American art critic to recommend her "not as a husband but as an enthusiastic admirer of her work, acid and tender, hard as steel and delicate and fine as a butterfly's wing, lovable as a beautiful smile, and profound and cruel as the bitterness of life."[6] Kahlo's support of Rivera's public art for the people was equally steadfast. In "Portrait of Diego," a lengthy essay she wrote in 1949 to accompany Rivera's fifty-year retrospective at the National Palace of Fine Arts, Kahlo penned an impassioned defense of his Communist ideals and "special adoration of the Indians" as "the living flower of the cultural tradition of the Americas."[7]

That Kahlo felt compelled to publicly defend her far more famous husband on the occasion of his state-sponsored retrospective reflects the complex relationship that both artists had to Marxist politics during their lifetime together. Before Rivera married Kahlo in 1929, he had managed to remain on the government payroll as a muralist and as a card-carrying Communist during a period when Mexico's post-revolutionary radicalism gave way to the consolidation of state power by conservative forces. By 1924, Vasconcelos had resigned as the Minister of Education and most of the artists he had commissioned to paint the walls of public buildings had been fired. Rivera survived the purge, despite the overt and contradictory political content of his murals. On one hand, his murals idealized Mexico's indigenous peoples and the Revolution's rural protagonists, whom his conservative critics derided as "Rivera's monkeys." On the other hand, they featured Soviet-style proletariat workers in overalls taking up arms against decadent capitalists. The former could only have been painted by an artist who had not witnessed the Revolution's devastation, the latter by a Communist whose belief in the revolutionary potential of the industrial masses took precedence over the historical reality of a Mexico whose impetus for social change lay in agrarian reform and the legacies of colonial oppression.

Rivera's remarkable juggling act of art and politics came to an end when he was expelled from the Communist Party in September 1929, just three weeks after he and Kahlo were married. The official reasons given for his expulsion were his acceptance of mural commissions from a government that, only months before, had declared the Communist Party illegal. As Rivera's new wife, Kahlo resigned from the Party in protest. Thereafter, they shared a revolutionary politics opposed to Joseph Stalin's ruthless grip of power over the Soviet Union and the international Communist Party. When Stalin's ideological adversary, Leon Trotsky, sought refuge in Mexico in the 1930s, Kahlo and Rivera sheltered him for two years at the Casa Azul. After Rivera and Trotsky quarreled in 1939, ostensibly over political differences and probably because of Kahlo's reputed affair with Trotsky, both artists renounced Trotsky and turned back to Stalin. Kahlo rejoined the Communist Party in 1948 at Rivera's urging, but Rivera was not readmitted until 1954, shortly after Kahlo died.

While Rivera and Kahlo's lifetime commitment to Communism was integral to their identity as artists, their political convictions did not deter them from strategically cultivating patrons and seeking celebrity status. For Rivera, this meant producing easel paintings and drawings in the 1920s to subsidize his meager pay as a muralist. In the early 1930s, it meant accepting commissions to paint murals for the millionaire industrialists of the United States, a nation Rivera deemed pivotal to a socialist future where technology and nature would be joined in harmony. In his Detroit Institute of the Arts mural cycle, commissioned by Edsel Ford, the industrial rhythm of autoworkers and the clenched fists of the four races of the world (European, American indigenous peoples, Asian, and African) have vanquished the breadlines and poverty of the Great Depression. In *Man Standing at the Crossroads*, the central figure of a worker stretches his arms to receive the fruits of science and the arts amidst the turmoil of war and revolution. When Nelson Rockefeller, who had commissioned this mural for the public lobby of New York City's Radio City building, demanded that Rivera remove a likeness of Lenin, he must have found Rivera's refusal to do so incomprehensible. Yet, for Rivera, a socialist future was unimaginable without Lenin standing on guard as the leader of the Russian Revolution, even if this resulted in Rockefeller suspending work on the mural in 1933 and ordering it destroyed the following year.

Although Rivera subsequently reproduced *Man Standing at the Crossroads* on a smaller scale in Mexico for the Palace of Fine Arts, the destruction of his original work deeply affected him as an artist. With the exception of his frescoes depicting the history of Mexico in the National Palace stairwell – which Rivera began in 1929 before leaving for the United States and finished after returning home to Mexico in 1934 – he would never again achieve the same degree of plasticity or synthesis of content in his murals. Nor did he obtain another mural commission in the United States until 1940, when he painted *Pan-American Unity* in San Francisco. In the 1940s and 1950s, he supported himself through commissioned portraits of patrons and children. He manifested his "special adoration of the Indians" by portraying *campesinos* bent over with flowers in his later paintings and rendering bucolic visions of a pre-Columbian past in his later murals.

Kahlo's political convictions found a different form of expression. She did not share Rivera's admiration for technology, perhaps because the trolley that shattered her body was heralded at the time as industrial progress, or because medicine could neither cure her spine nor save her from miscarriages or the amputation of her right foot the year before she died. Nor did she idealize Mexico's indigenous peoples. Instead, she derived her inspiration from popular culture, where to dress as an Indigenous Tehuana woman in Mexico City was to signify overt sexuality rather than humble modesty, and to make small paintings was to reference the tradition of anonymous *ex-votos* and *retablos* asking the Virgin Mary for divine intervention or recording some tragedy, such as Kahlo's portrayal of her Detroit miscarriage in *Henry Ford Hospital*. While Rivera's synthesis of indigenous and European cultures looked outward to represent the rural protagonists of the Mexican Revolution, Kahlo's embrace of the transformative values of *mestizaje* turned inward to reflect upon her dual heritage. For Rivera, nature was aligned in harmony with an indigenous universe and represented by flowers; in Kahlo's self-portraits, it oscillates between parched earth and enveloping vegetation. Where Rivera idolized the revolutionary masses, Kahlo kept company with animals and dolls.

Yet despite these differences in their creative visions – his expansive and historical, hers internal and personal – Kahlo's lifetime commitment to Communism was no less passionate than Rivera's. Large portraits of Communist leaders hung in her bedroom in the Casa Azul, where Kahlo resided from 1939 until her death in 1954. Her painting *Marxism Heals the Sick* attests to her faith in a socialist future, which sustained her battles with chronic pain as much as it sustained her bond with Diego. Of her many masks, Communism was not one of them. It lay behind the persona she created, keeping her company in the darkness of the night when her elaborate costumes were stripped from her body and replaced by corsets. It led her to disobey her doctor's orders and leave her sickbed to demonstrate against the overthrow of Guatemala's socialist president by a CIA-engineered coup only weeks before she died. For Kahlo, as for Rivera, politics embodied the quest to realize a "vision of the truth" for an art of Mexico and of the people.

While the great revolutionary upheavals that shaped Rivera's and Kahlo's Marxist beliefs and passion for Mexican culture are now shrouded in history, what belongs to the present is the legacy of their creative vision. Their spirit lives on in the social panorama of Rivera's public murals and Kahlo's riveting gaze in her diminutive self-portraits; it comes alive in the Casa Azul, preserved as a memorial to their years spent together inside its garden walls; it persists through their own writings and of those who knew them well. Bertram Wolfe describes what a strange couple they made when they first met:

> This frail, slender, dynamic girl with her colorful raiment, jewels, ribbons, and make-up resembling some pre-Conquest Indian princess, with the ribbons in her hair barely coming up to her male companion's shoulder, accompanying this lumbering giant of a frog-faced man in a huge sombrero, ill-fitting tweeds, or paint-stained overalls. . . . Yet nobody laughed at their unusual appearance; even those who had never seen their pictures nor heard their names felt that they were contemplating an extraordinary pair.[8]

By the end of their lives, the confluence of passion and politics had made Kahlo's and Rivera's art as extraordinary as their pairing.

1. Diego Rivera (with Gladys March), *My Art, My Life: An Autobiography* (New York: Citadel Books, 1960. Reprinted by Dover Books, 1991), p. 79.
2. Kahlo quoted in "Mexican Autobiography," *Time* (April 27, 1953).
3. *The Diary of Frida Kahlo: An Intimate Self-Portrait* (New York: Abrams, 2005), pp. 282–83.
4. Rivera, *My Art, My Life*, p. 50.
5. Kahlo quoted in Hayden Herrera, *Frida: A Biography of Frida Kahlo* (New York: Harper & Row, 1983), p. 266. For Rivera's version, see Rivera, *My Art, My Life*, p. 103.
6. Bertram D. Wolfe, *The Fabulous Life of Diego Rivera* (New York: Stein and Day, 1963. Reprinted by Scarborough Books, 1990), p. 360.
7. *Frida by Frida: Selection of Letters and Texts by Rachel Tibol*, translated by Gregory Dechant (Mexico: Editorial RM, 2006), p. 356.
8. Wolfe, *The Fabulous Life of Diego Rivera*, p. 396.

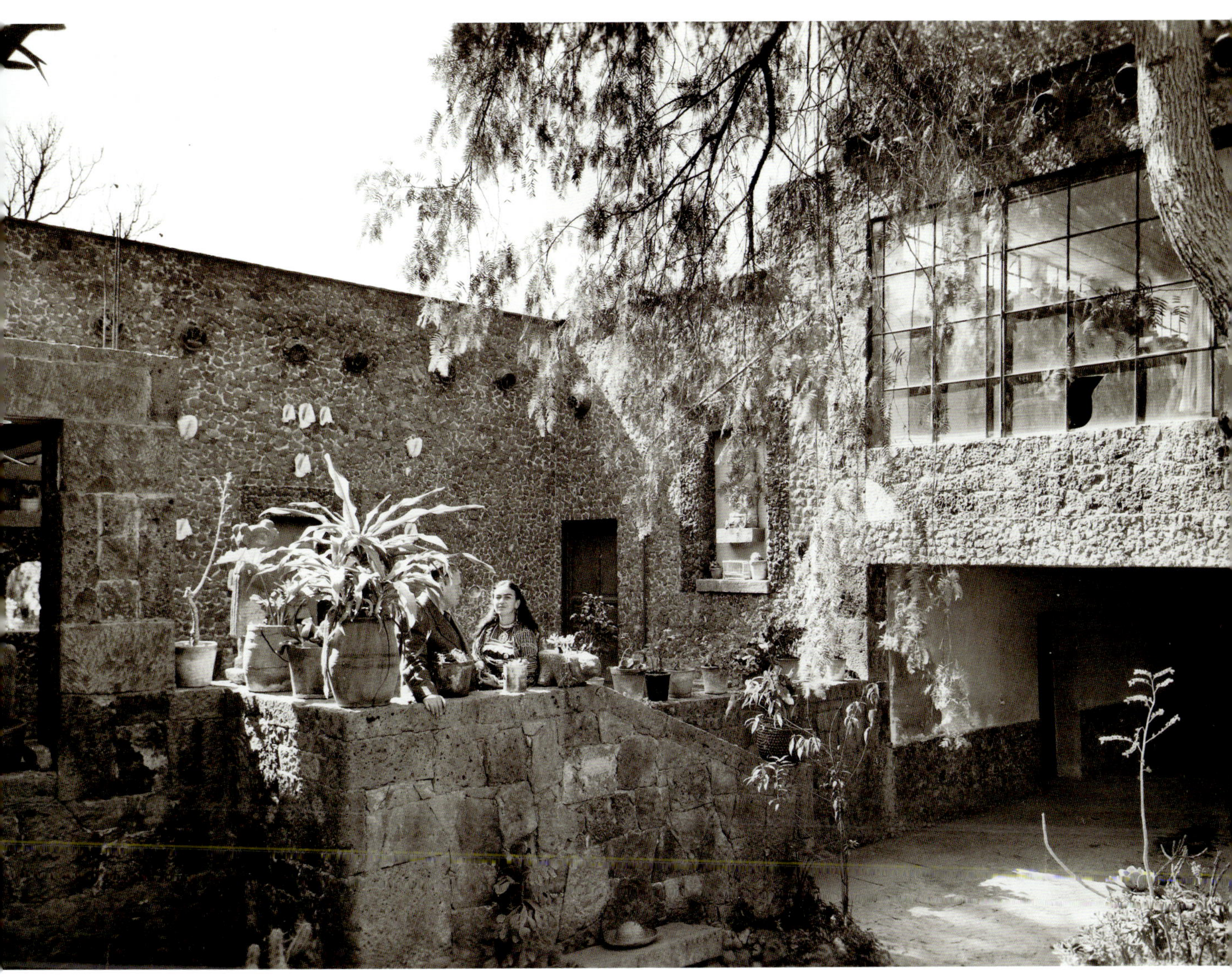

Guillermo Zamora, *Diego and Frida in the Casa Azul*, c. 1952

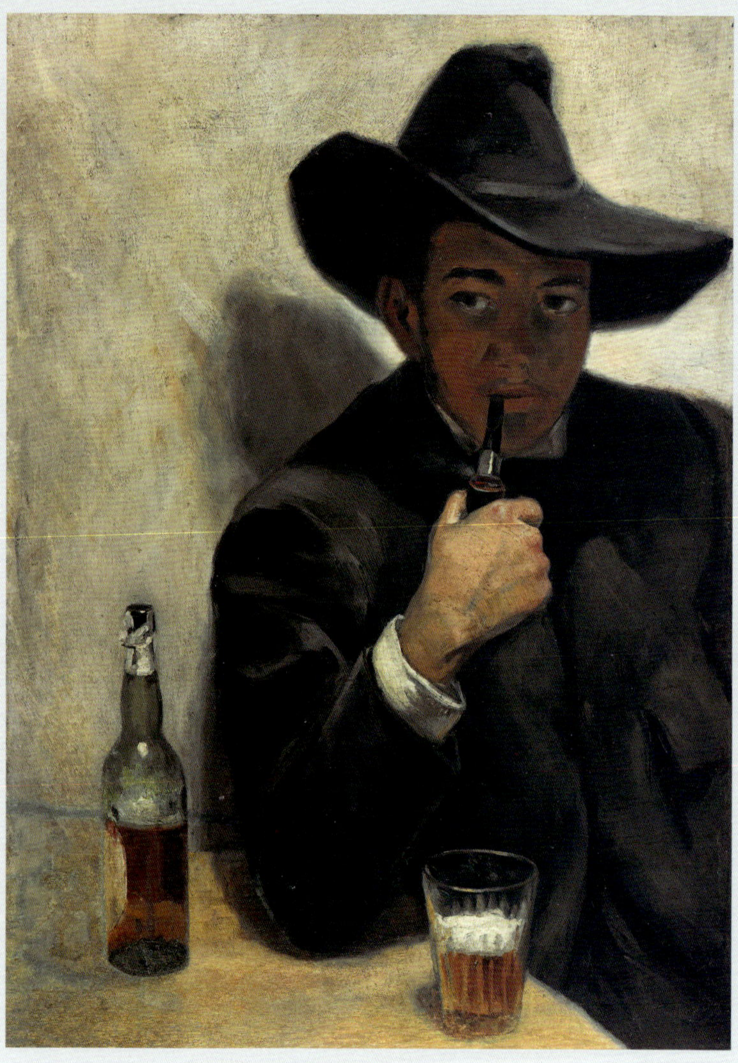

European Influences

Through the sponsorship of Teodoro A. Dehesa Méndez, governor of the state of Veracruz, Diego Rivera traveled from Mexico City to Madrid in 1907 at the age of twenty-one to continue his artistic studies with the esteemed Realist painter Eduardo Chicharro y Agüera, whose stylistic influence can be seen in *Self-Portrait with Wide-Brimmed Hat* and *The Bullfighter*. Rivera's style became more experimental after he moved to Paris in 1909. There he immersed himself in the avant-garde circles of Montparnasse. When Rivera's grant expired in 1910, he supported himself through sales of his paintings, which enabled him to remain in Europe for the next decade. From 1913 to 1917, he adopted the aesthetic of analytic Cubism. In 1917, his style shifted yet again to a post-Impressionist mode inspired by Paul Cézanne's still lifes, bringing about a return to figurative painting. By 1919, having worked through his experiments with Cubism, Rivera reverted to a more Realist aesthetic, as seen in *The Mathematician*. His Cubist period had a marked influence on his later work, specifically in the spatial density that would characterize his murals.

▲ Diego Rivera *Self-Portrait with Wide-Brimmed Hat*, 1907

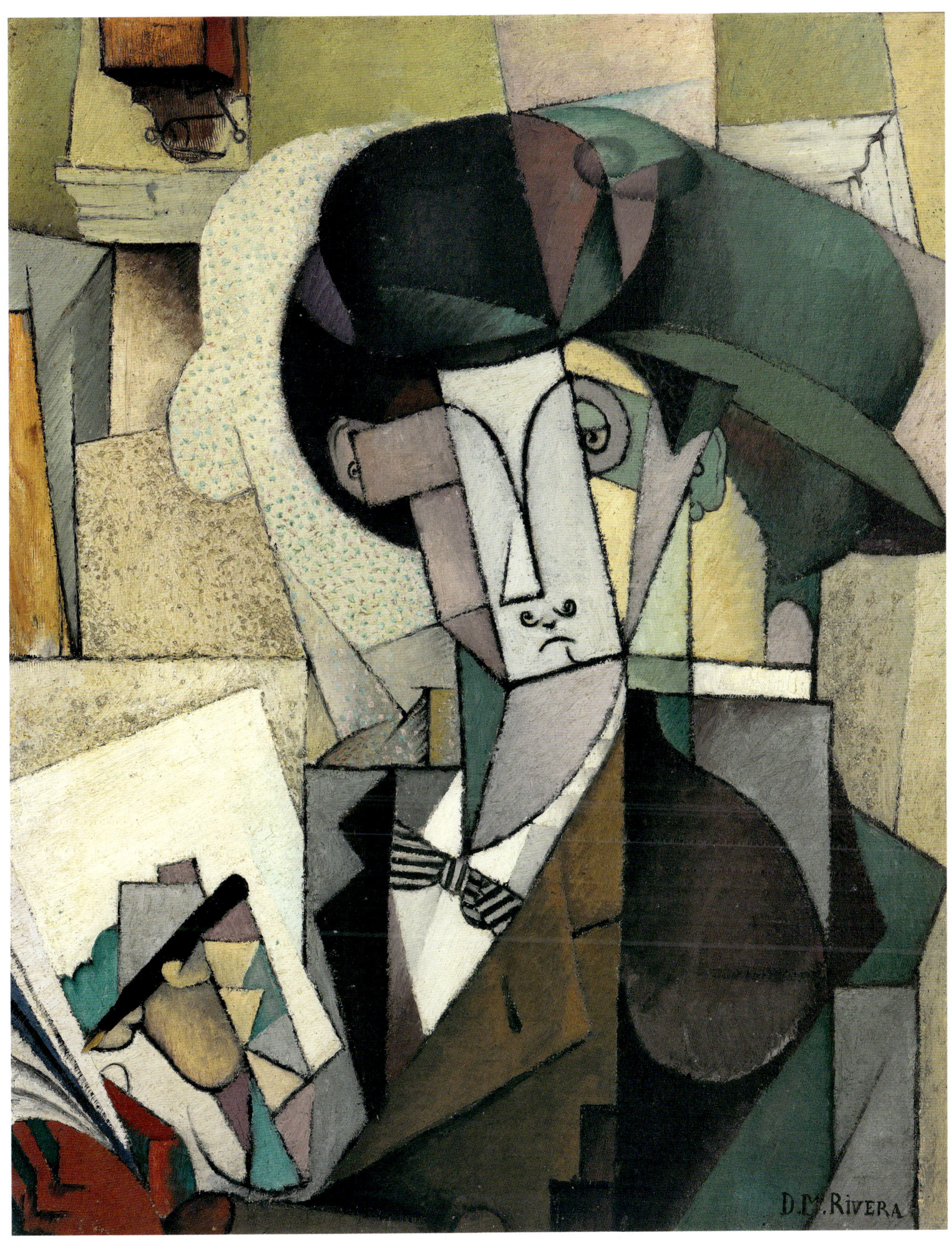

Diego Rivera *Young Man with a Fountain Pen (Portrait of Best Maugard)*, 1914

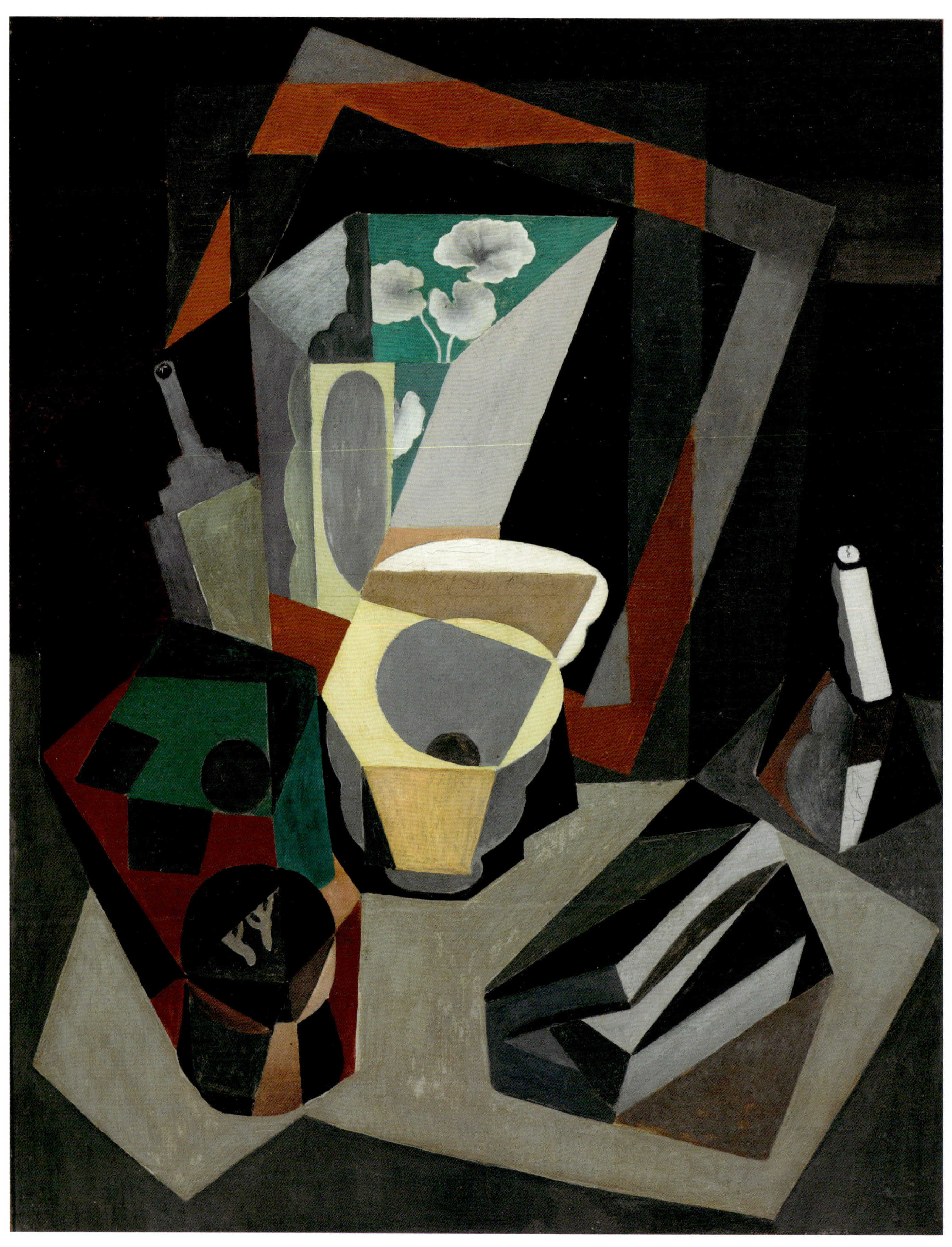

Diego Rivera *Still Life with Plant*, 1917

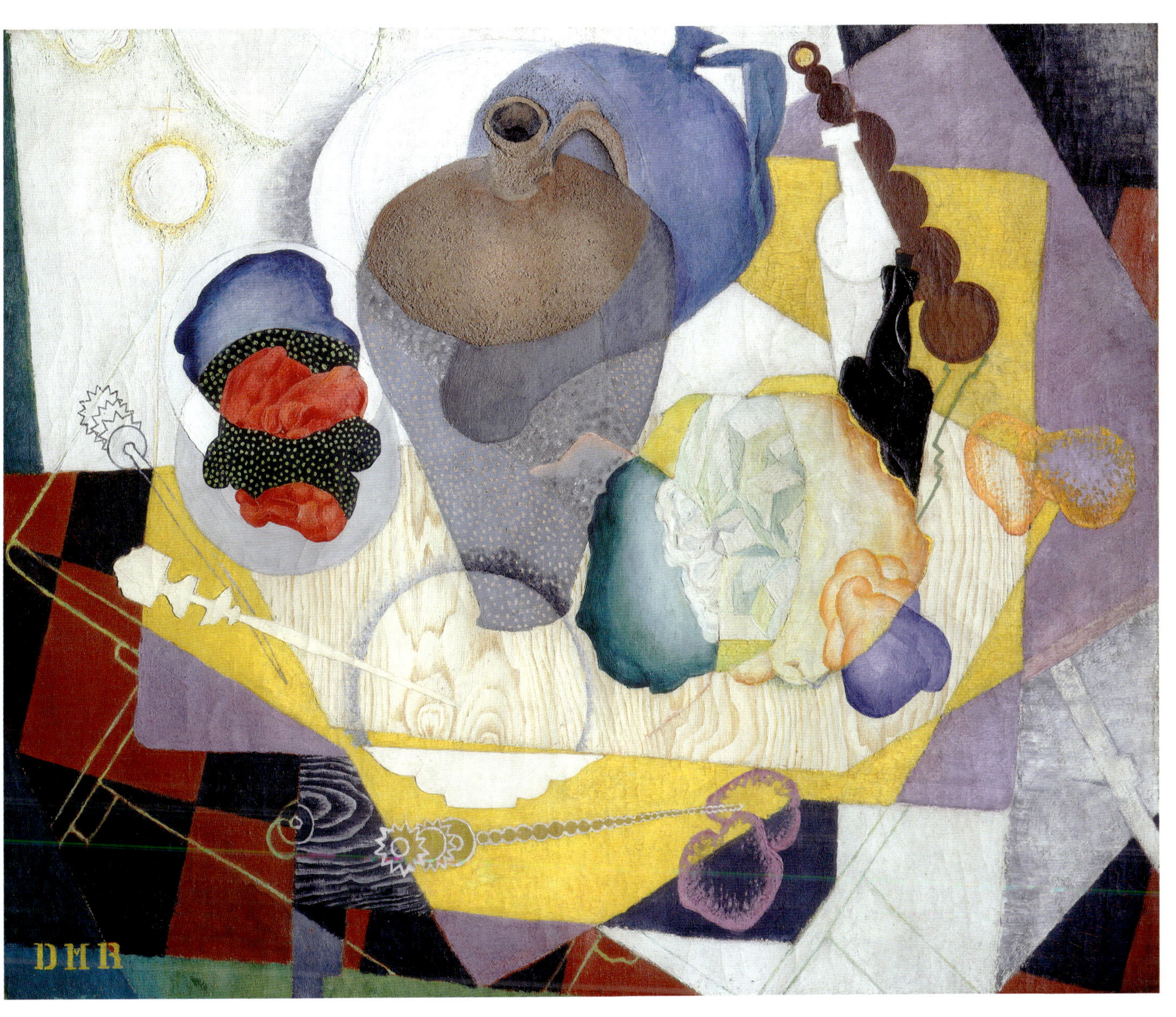

▲ Diego Rivera *Spanish Still Life, No. 9*, 1915

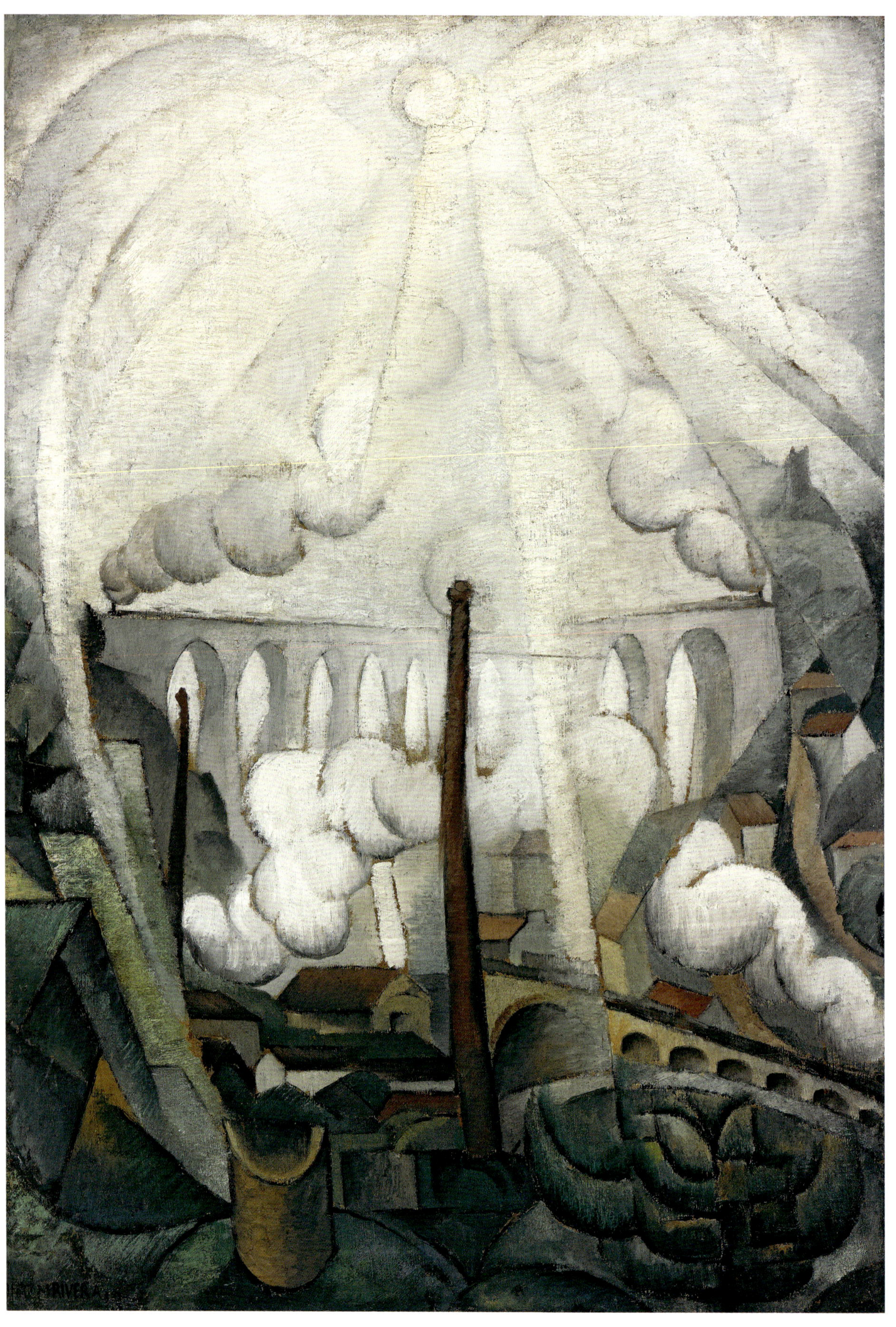

Diego Rivera *Sun Breaking through the Mist (The Road to Meudon)*, 1913

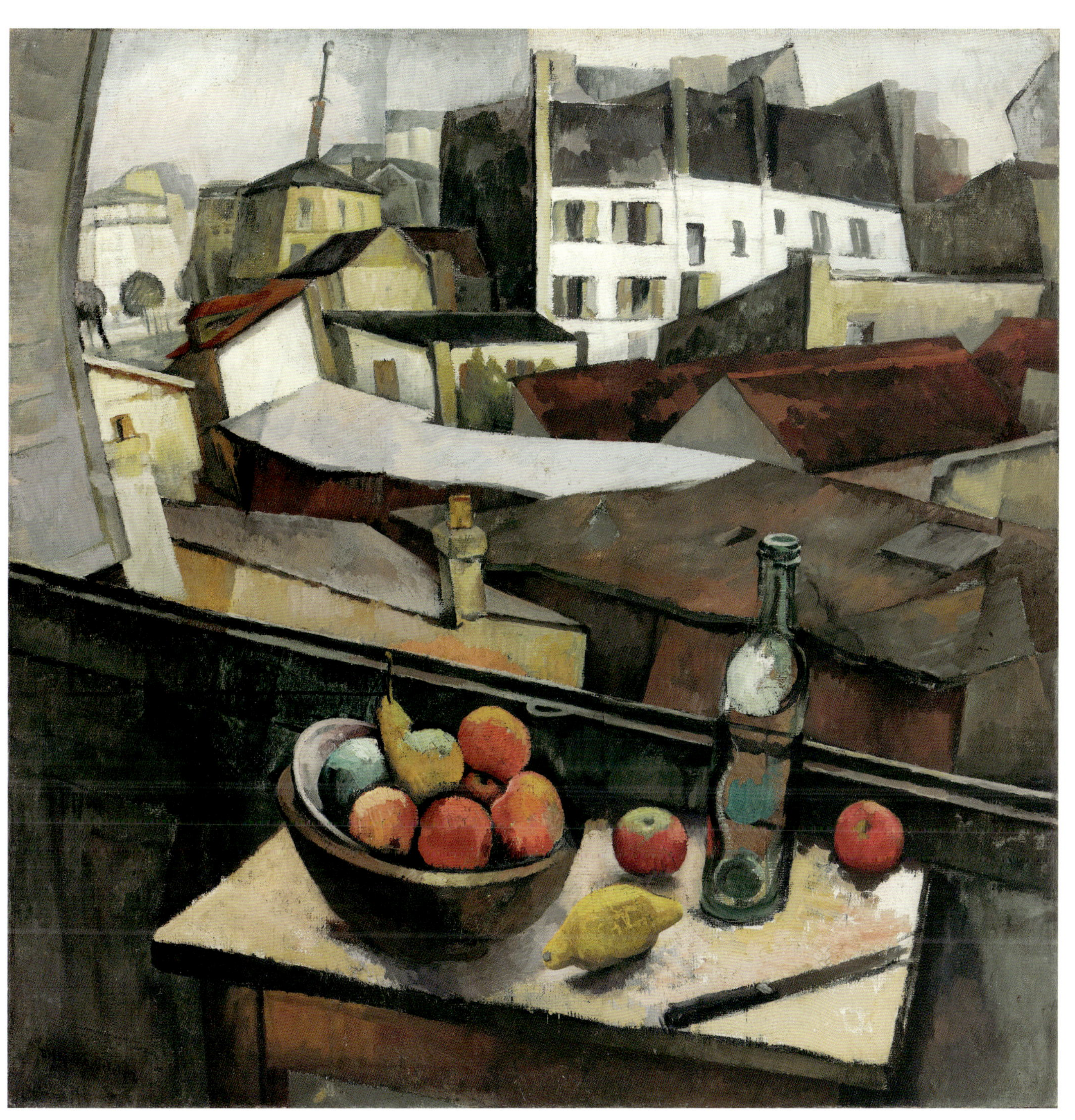

Diego Rivera *Knife and Fruit in Front of the Window*, 1917

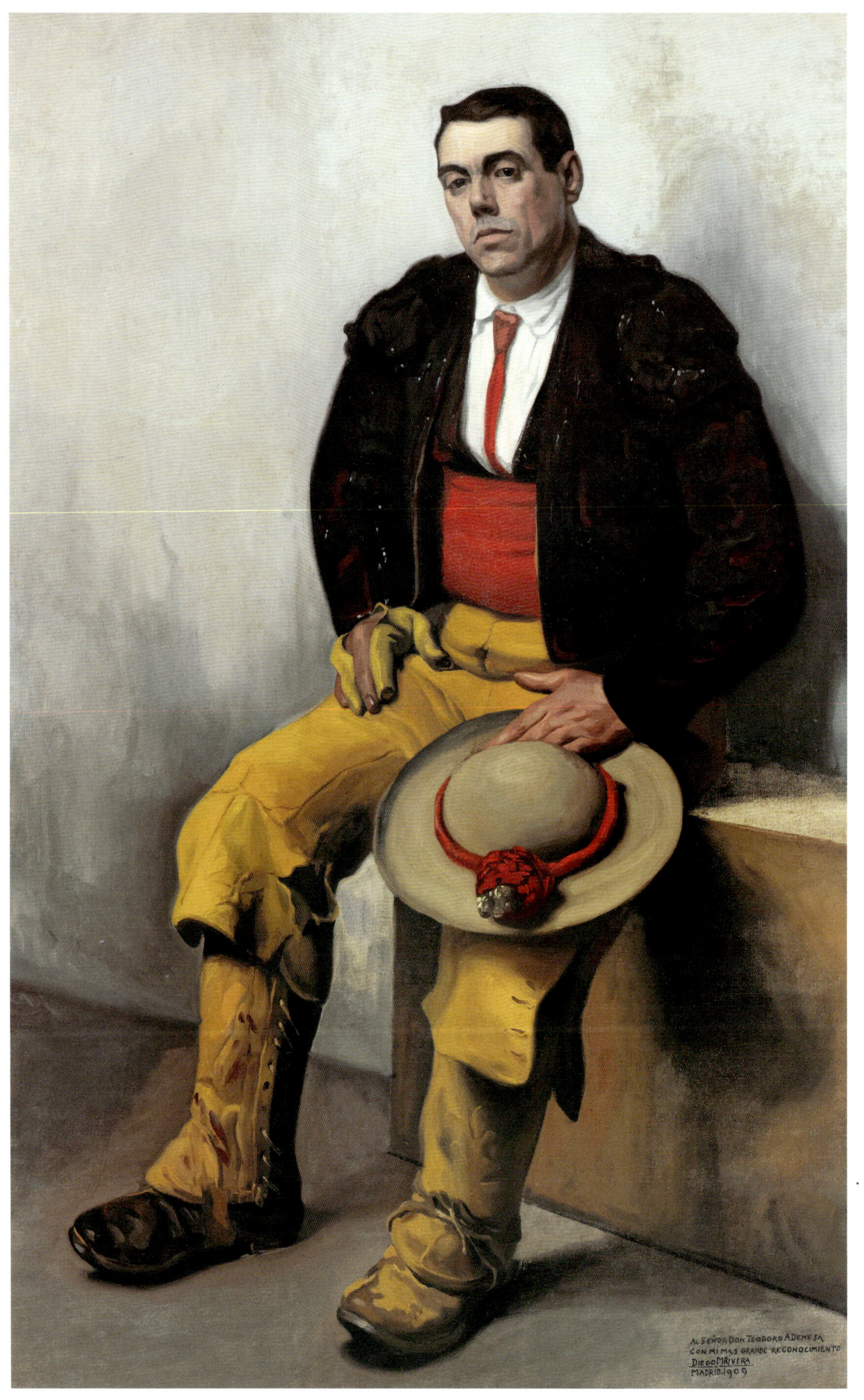

Diego Rivera *The Bullfighter*, 1909

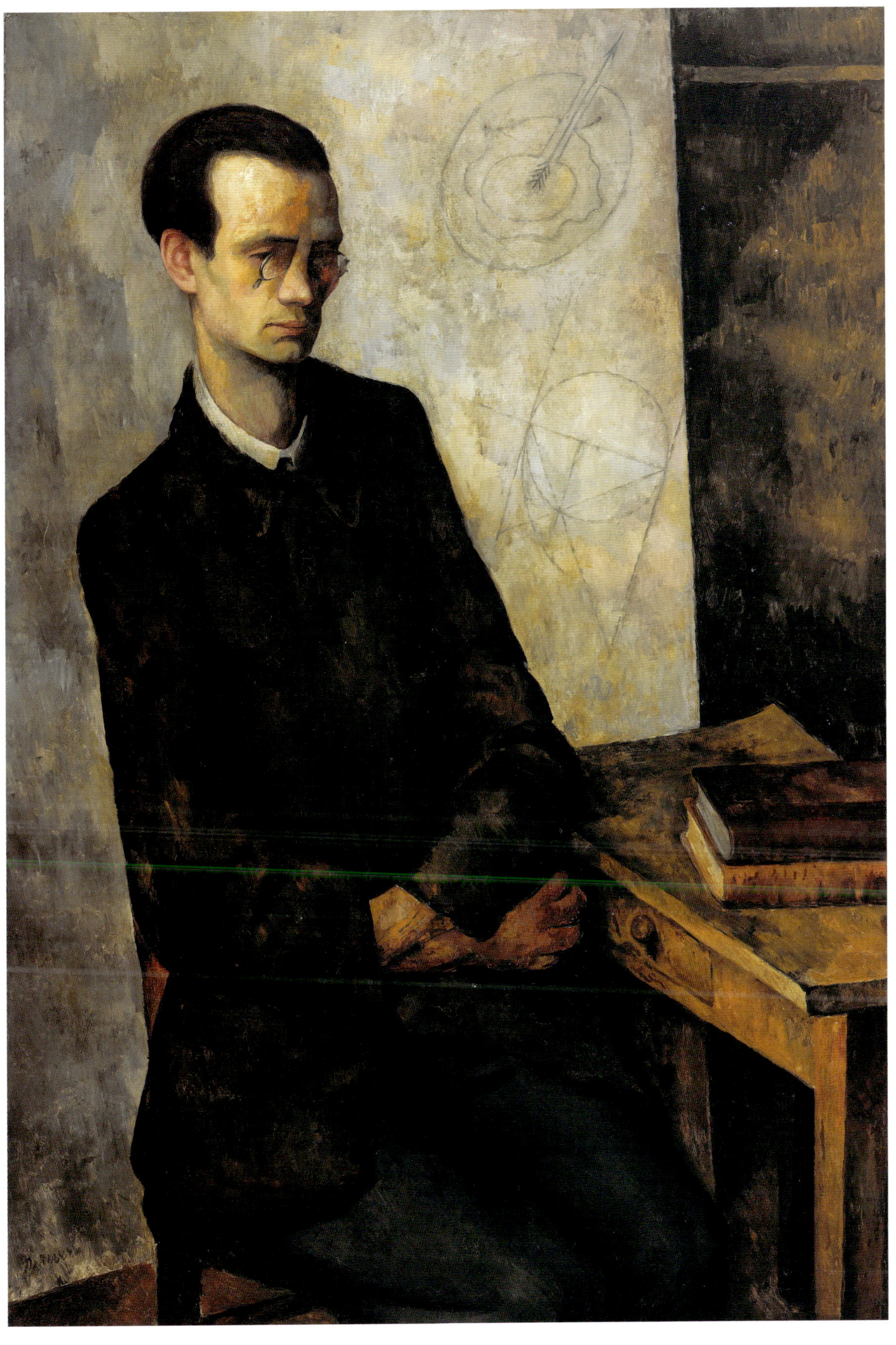

Diego Rivera *The Mathematician*, 1919

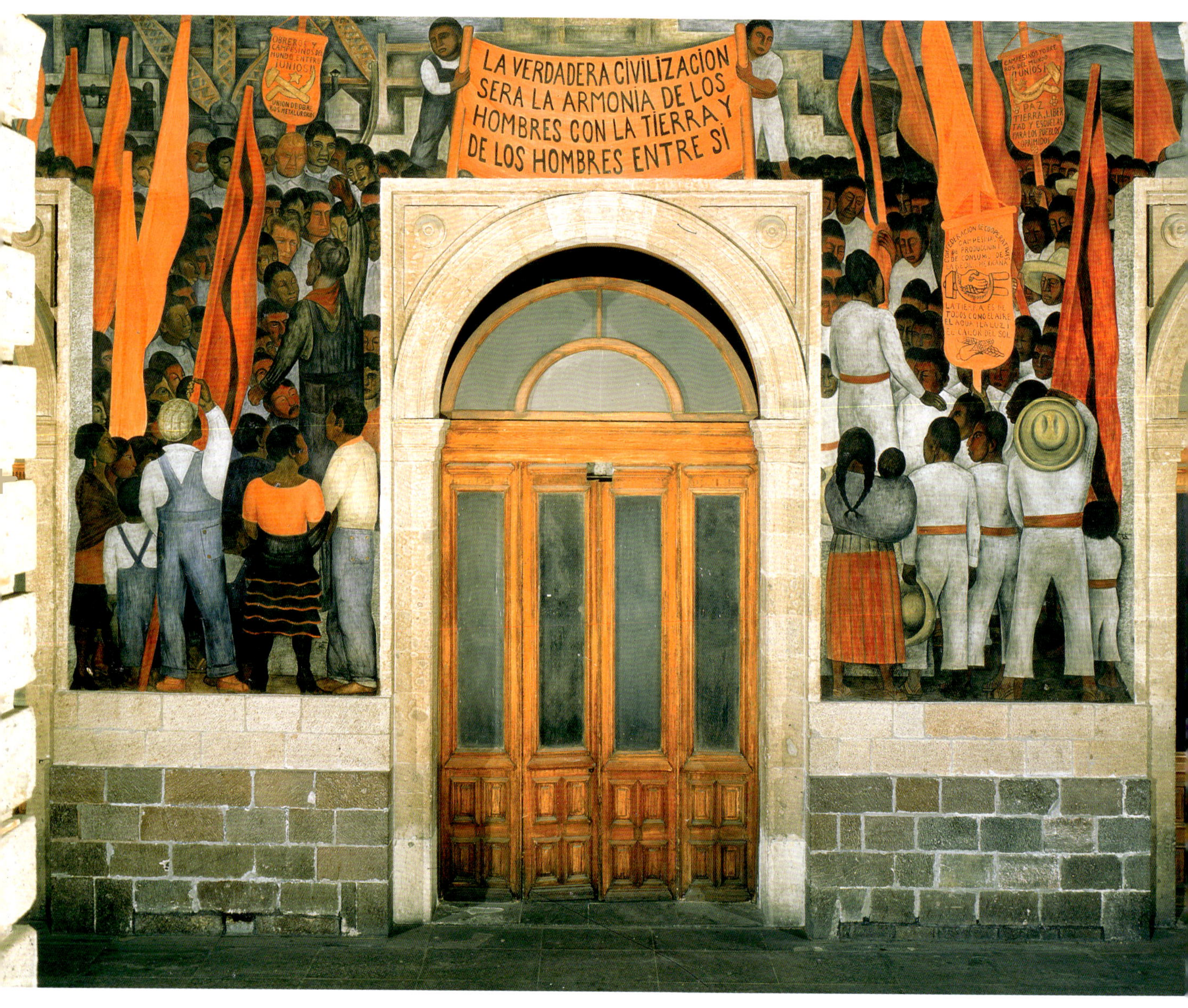

▲ Diego Rivera *Assembly*, 1923–1924

Manifesto of the Union of Technical Workers, Painters, and Sculptors
(issued as a broadside in Mexico City in 1923 and published in *El Machete* in 1924)

To the indigenous peoples humiliated for centuries; to the common soldiers made executioners by their chiefs; to workers and peasants scourged by the greed of the rich; to intellectuals uncorrupted by the bourgeoisie:

…

Not only are our people (especially our indigenous people) the source of all that is noble toil, all that is virtue, but also, every manifestation of the physical and spiritual existence of our nation as an ethnic force springs from them. So does the extraordinary and marvelous ability to create beauty. *The art of the Mexican people is the most important and vital spiritual expression in the world today, and its indigenous traditions lie at its very heart*. It is great precisely because it is of the people and therefore collective. That is why our primary aesthetic aim is to promote art that will help destroy all traces of bourgeois individualism. We repudiate so-called easel painting and all the ultra-intellectual salon art of the aristocracy and exalt the manifestation of monumental art.

…

We believe that while our society is in a transitional stage between the destruction of an old order and the introduction of a new order, the creators of beauty must turn their work into clear ideological propaganda for the people, and make art something of beauty, education, and purpose.

…

We are sure that the victory of the working classes will bring a harmonious flowering of art of cosmological and historical significance to our race, comparable to that of our wonderful ancient indigenous civilizations. *We will fight tirelessly to bring this about*.

…

For the proletariat of the world:

Secretary-General, David Alfaro Siqueiros
Committee member, Diego Rivera
Committee member, Xavier Guerrero

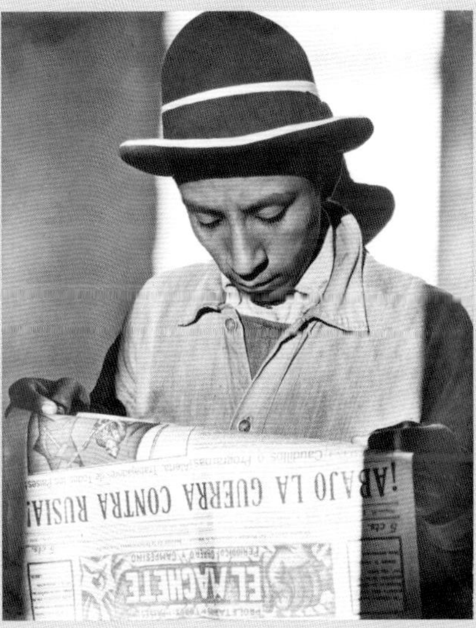

Tina Modotti, *Worker Reading* El Machete, 1927

Excerpted and adapted from the English translation of the Manifesto in Dawn Ades, *Art in Latin America* (New Haven and London: Yale University Press, 1989), p. 324.

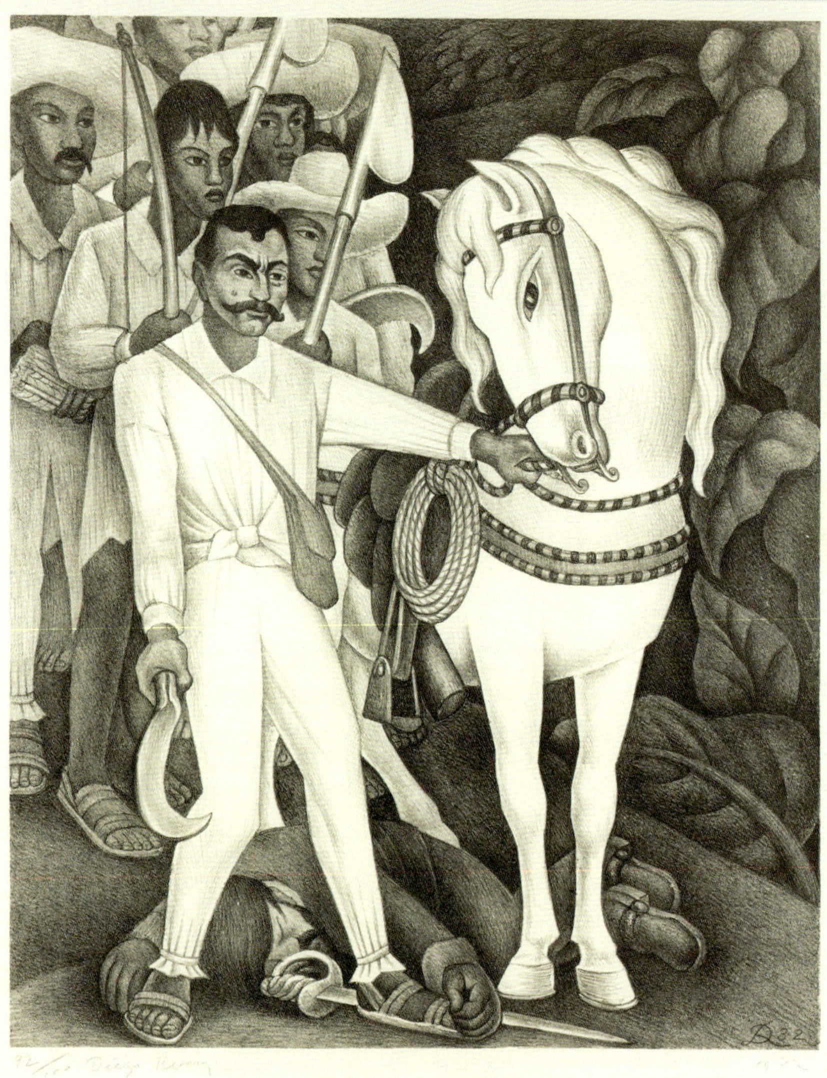

Mexican Muralism

With the end of the Mexican Revolution (1910–1920), José Vasconcelos, the Minister of Education, embarked on an ambitious program of sponsoring public art that made Mexico the centre of a muralist renaissance in the 1920s. Of the many artists who painted Mexico's walls during this period, Diego Rivera, José Clemente Orozco, and David Alfaro Siqueiros were the most famous. Siqueiros and Orozco adopted an expressionist style in their murals and derived their inspiration from Mexico's graphic art traditions. By contrast, Rivera drew upon his studies of Italian Renaissance frescoes and pre-Columbian art to produce murals that idealized indigenous culture and rural revolutionaries such as Emiliano Zapata. After Rivera traveled to the Soviet Union in 1927, his murals became more overtly political but no less utopian in their depiction of revolutionary struggle.
Of the three muralists, Rivera was the most adept at obtaining government and private patronage. Rivera's artistic ambitions were often at odds with his espousal of Marxist politics, resulting in his expulsion from the Communist Party in 1929 and the rupture of his friendship with Siqueiros, who together with Rivera issued the Manifesto of the Union of Technical Workers, Painters, and Sculptors in 1923.

▲ Diego Rivera *The Agrarian Leader Zapata*, 1932

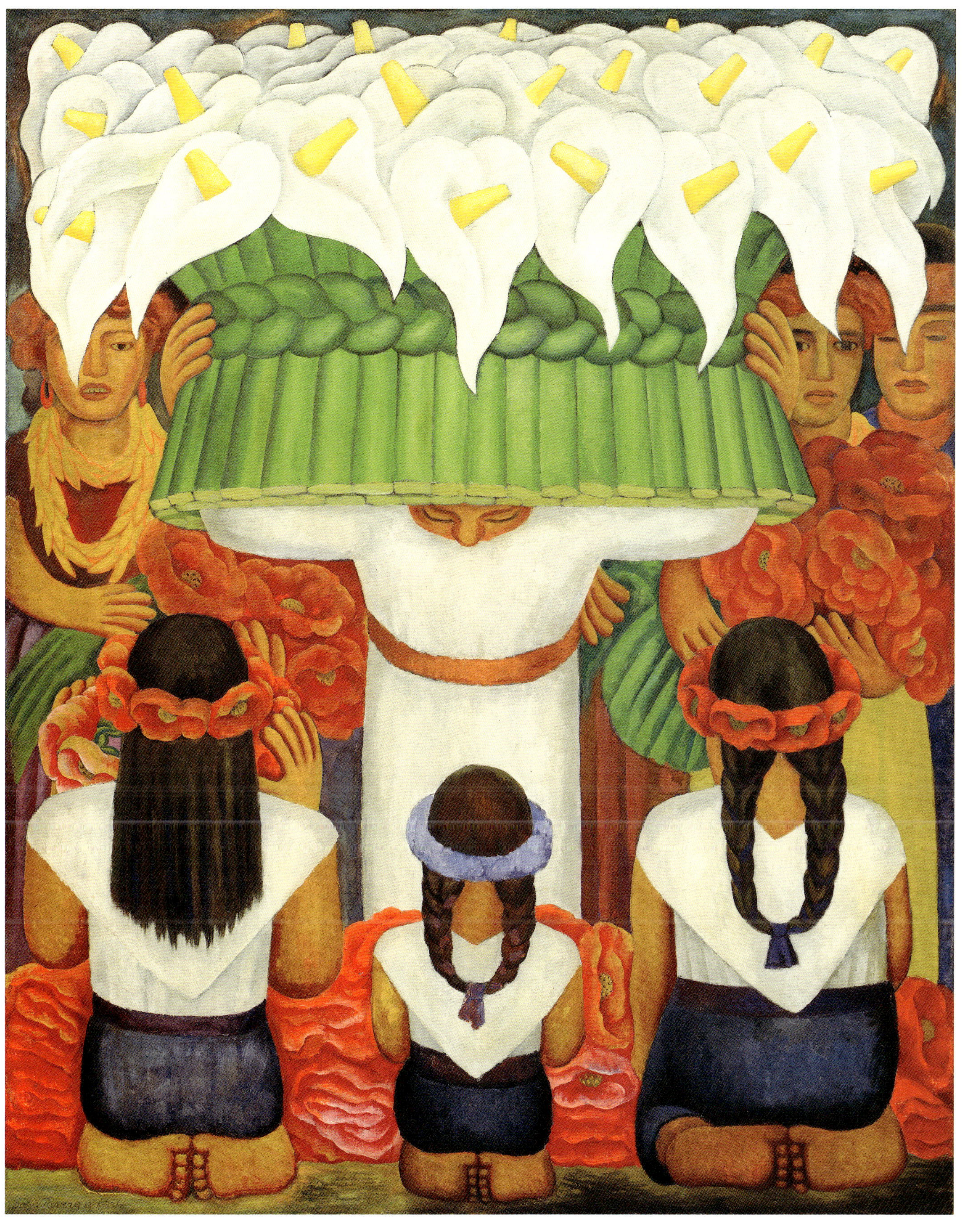

▲ Diego Rivera *Flower Festival: Feast of Santa Anita*, 1931

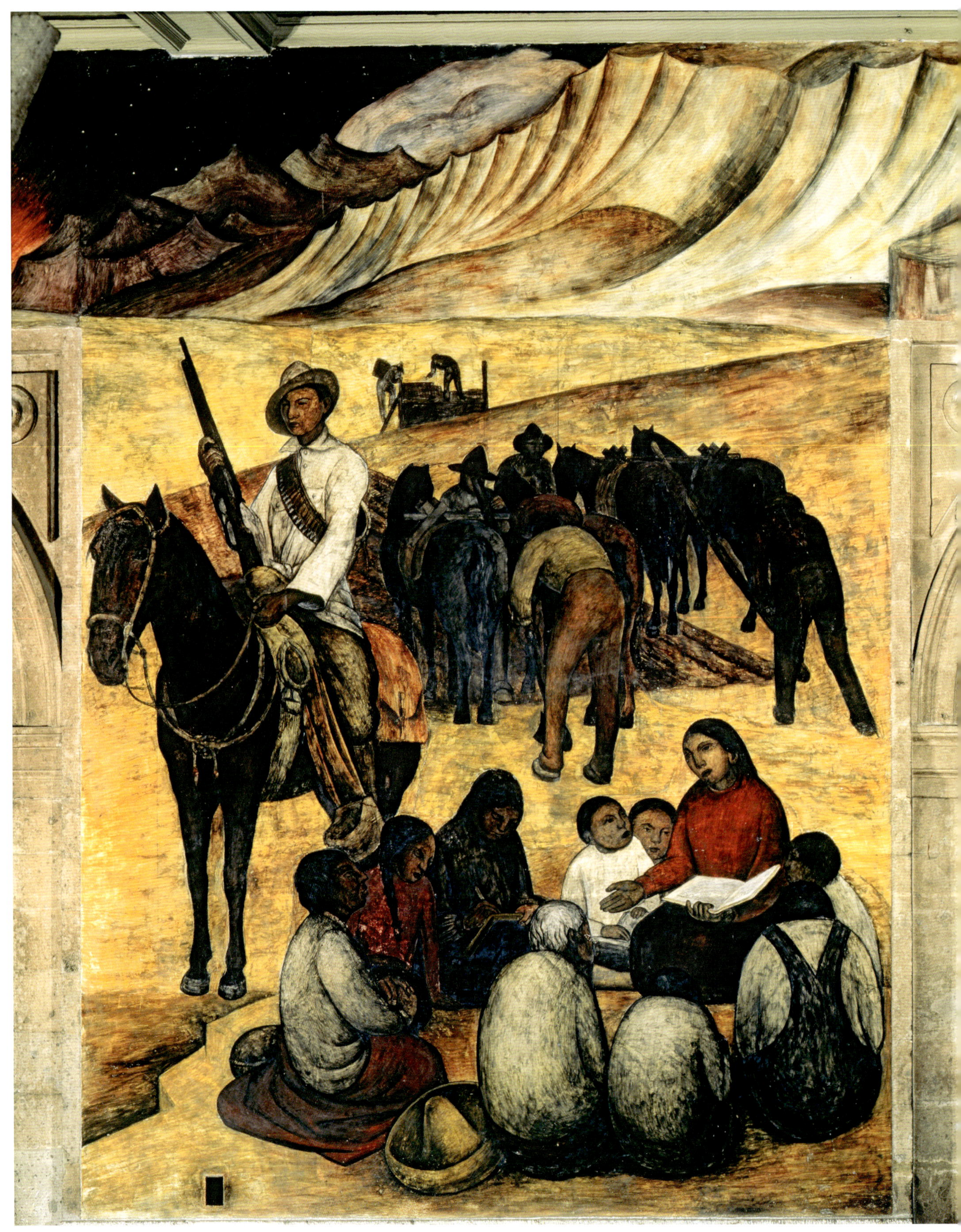

▲ Diego Rivera *The Rural Schoolteacher*, 1923–1924

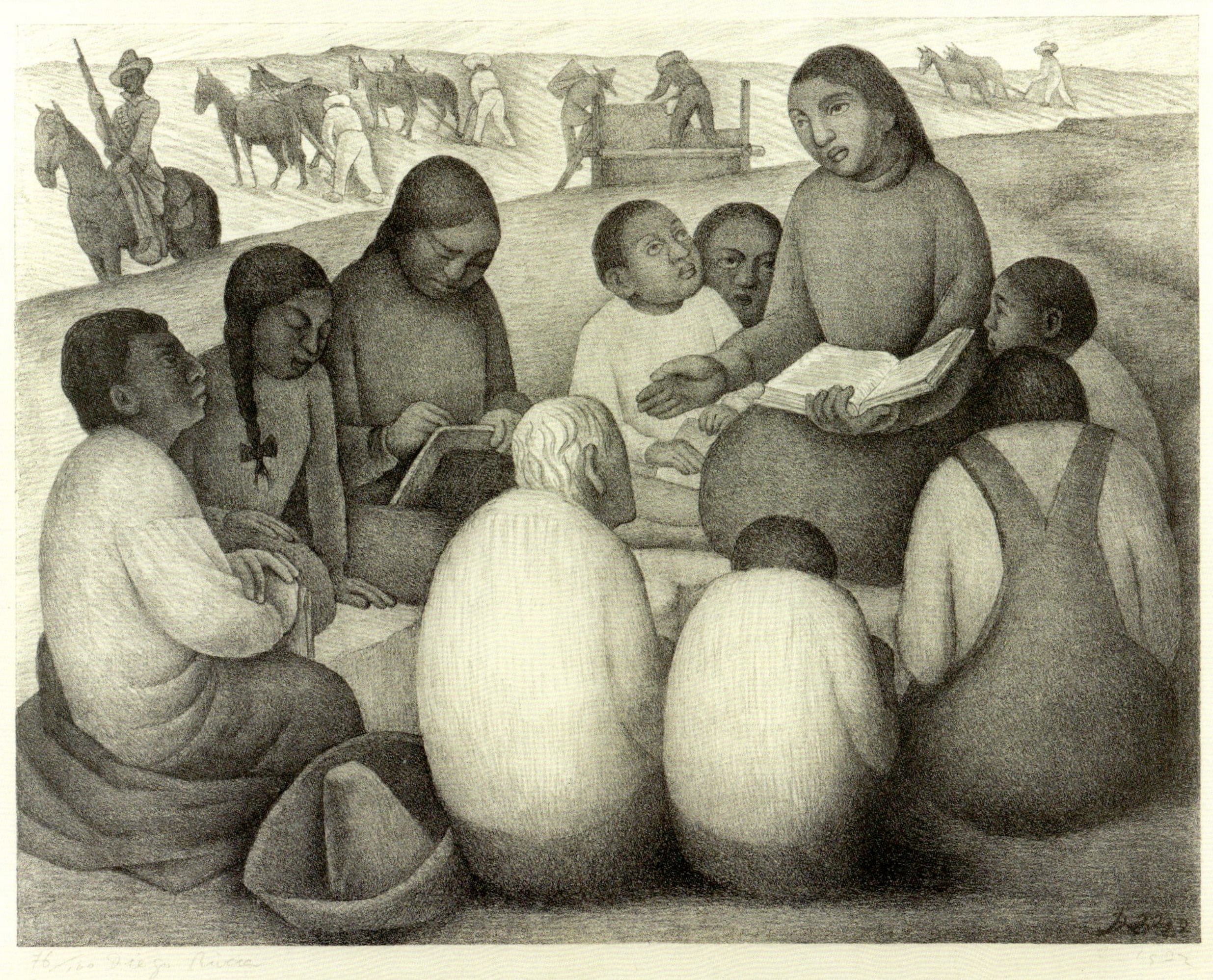

The Ministry of Education Frescoes

Diego Rivera achieved his international acclaim as a muralist while painting the courtyard walls of the Ministry of Education in the 1920s. Details from these murals were often featured in his later lithographs and paintings. Rivera's first mural cycle at the Ministry was painted in 1923–1924. It featured scenes from rural life in Mexico, including labour activities such as pottery making, sugar grinding, and mining; traditional indigenous dances; and popular festivals such as the Day of the Dead. This cycle also depicted the post-revolutionary politics of distributing land to rural workers, union organizing, and literacy campaigns. In 1928–1929, Rivera returned to the Ministry of Education to paint a series of frescoes that were influenced by his previous year's travels to the Soviet Union. Titled *Ballad of the Proletarian Revolution/Ballad of the Agrarian Revolution*, this mural cycle featured a utopian vision of Marxist ideology being imparted to rural workers. In Rivera's best-known fresco from this cycle, *The Arsenal* (see page 40), Frida Kahlo is featured in the centre distributing arms to the people, while Tina Modotti, the Italian-American photographer, is standing on the far right holding a cartridge of bullets. The muralist David Alfaro Siqueiros, wearing a hat emblazoned with the red star, peers over the shoulder of an armed proletarian worker.

▲ Diego Rivera *The Rural Schoolteacher*, 1932

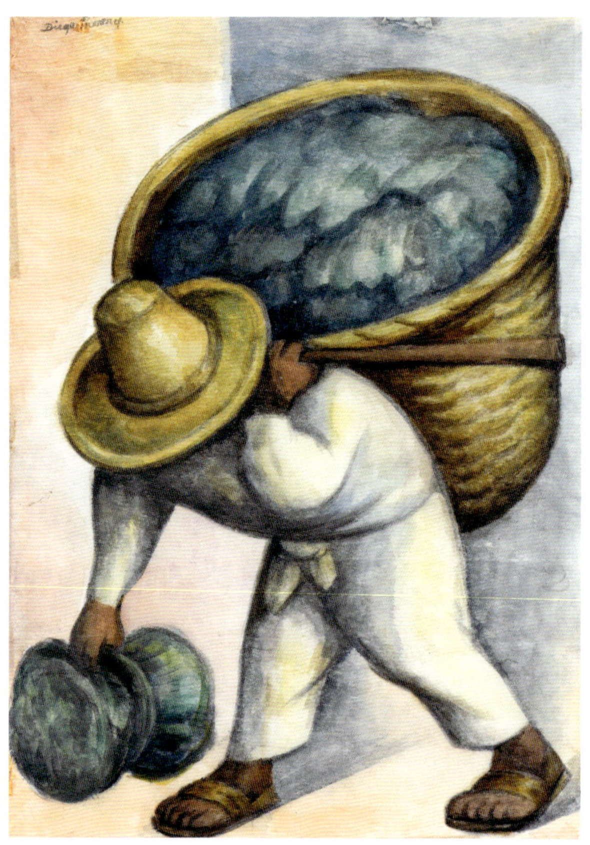

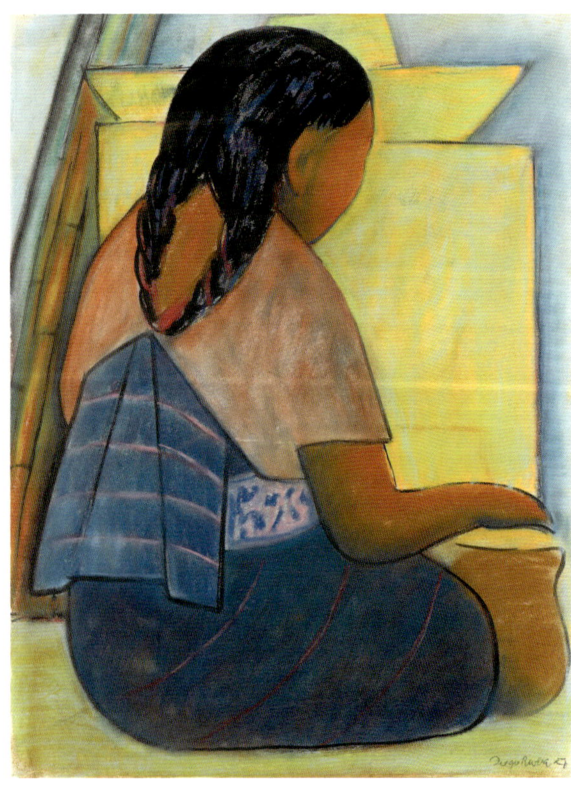

▲ Diego Rivera *Woman Grinding Corn*, 1927

▲▲ Diego Rivera *Cabbage Seller*, 1936

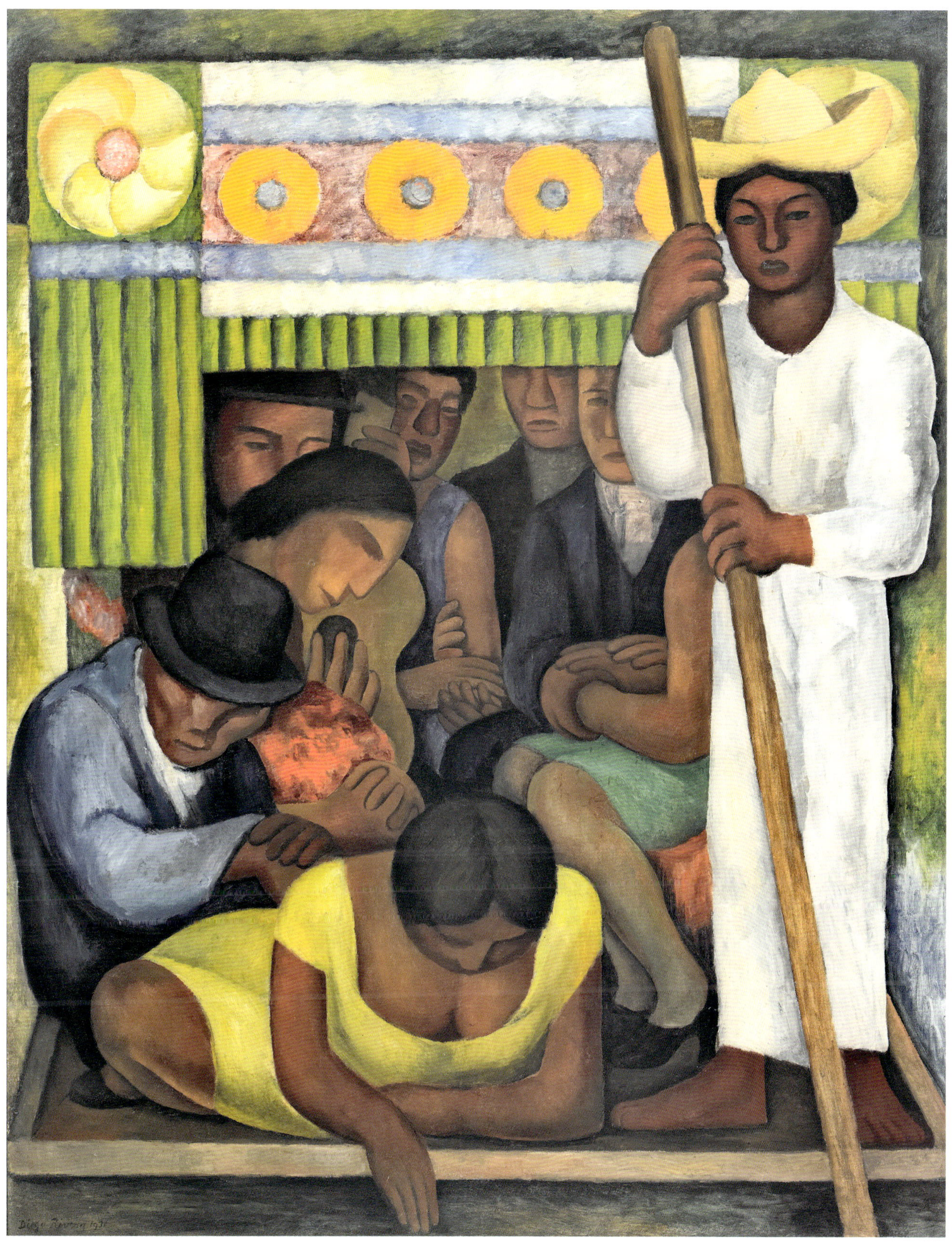

Diego Rivera *The Flowered Canoe*, 1931

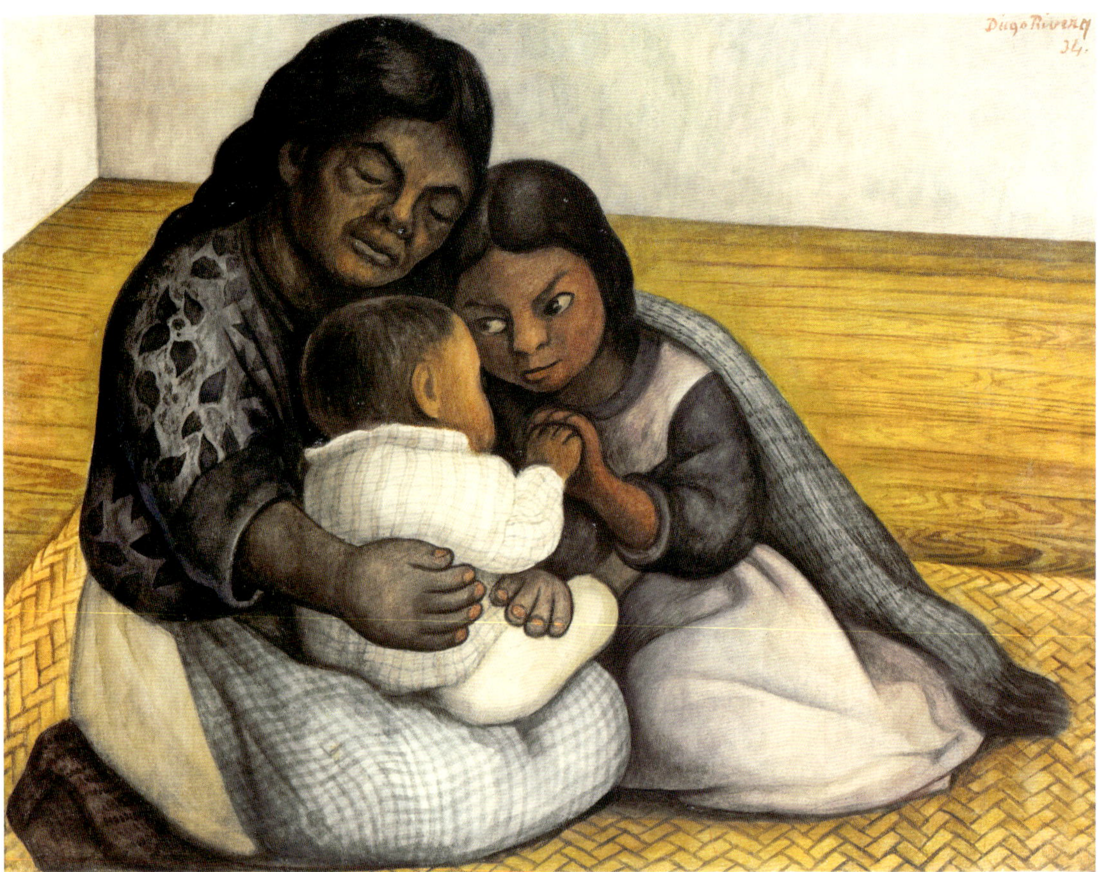

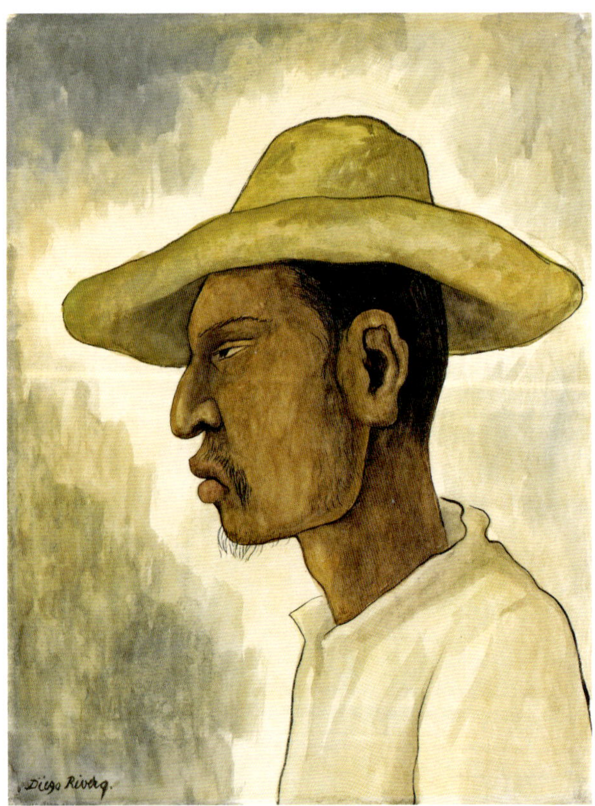

▲ Diego Rivera *Head*, c. 1936

▲▲ Diego Rivera *The Family (Mother and Children)*, 1934

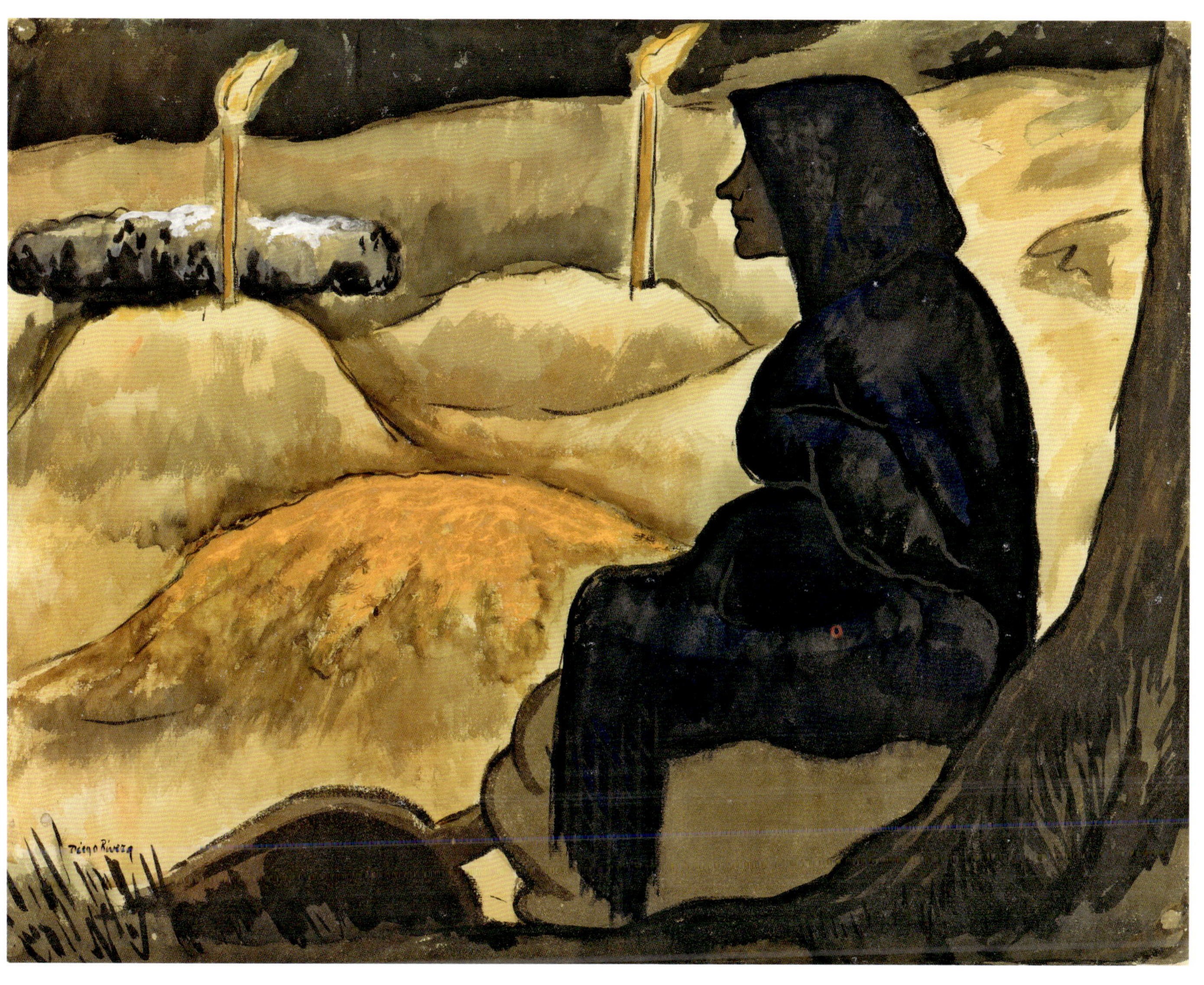

▲ Diego Rivera *Day of the Dead*, c. 1936

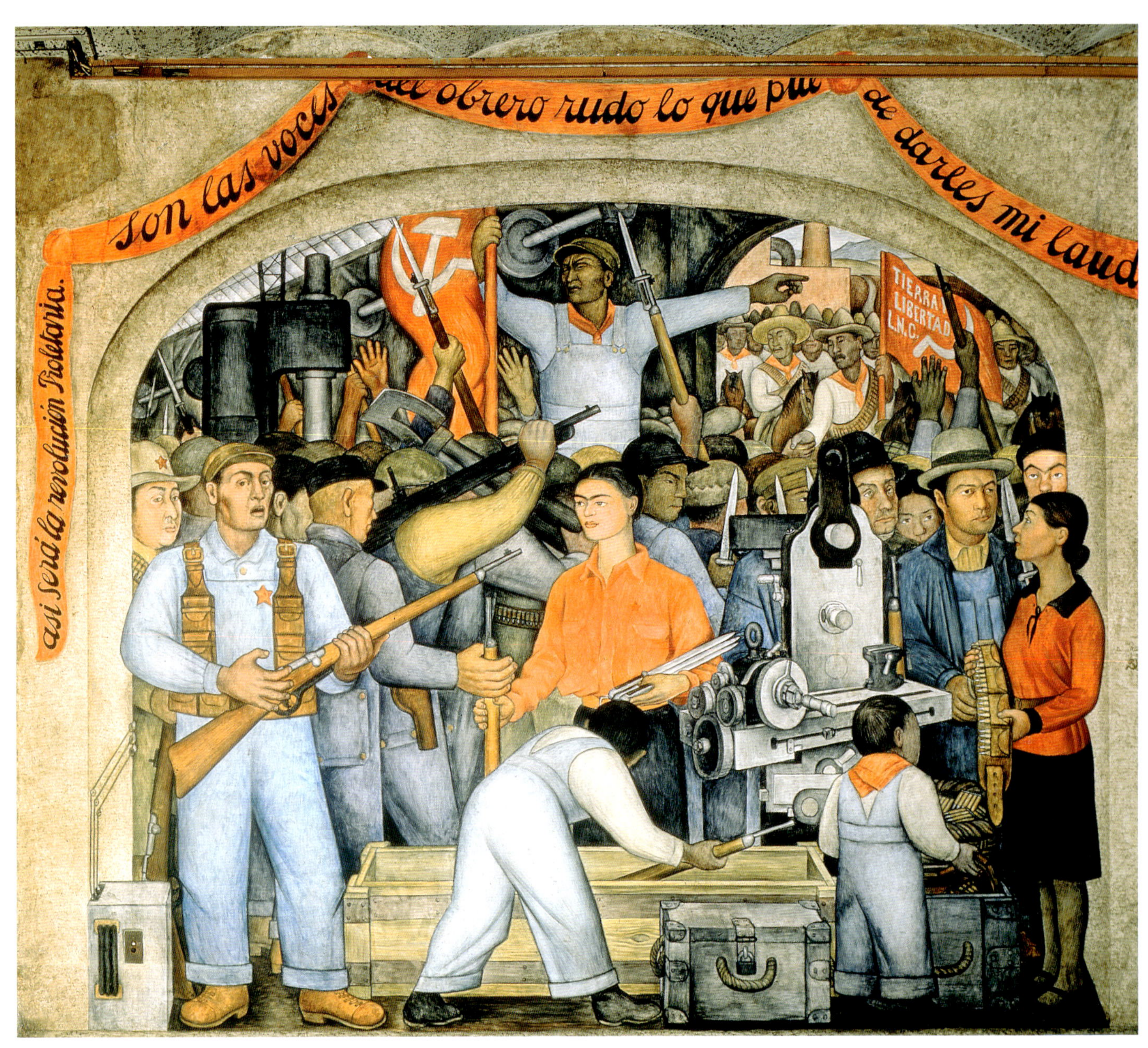

▲ Diego Rivera *The Arsenal*, 1928–1929

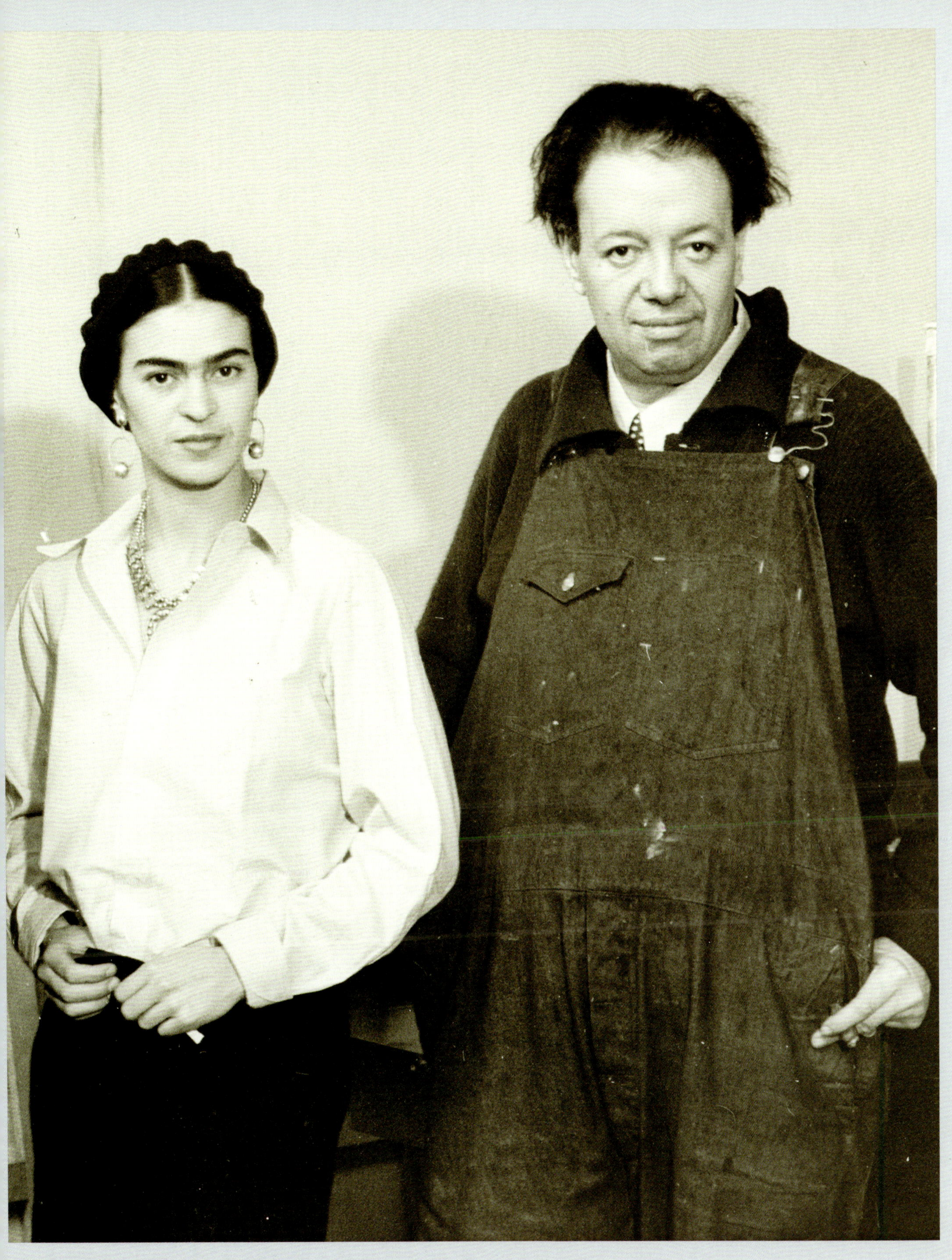

Anonymous, *Frida Kahlo and Diego Rivera*, c. 1933

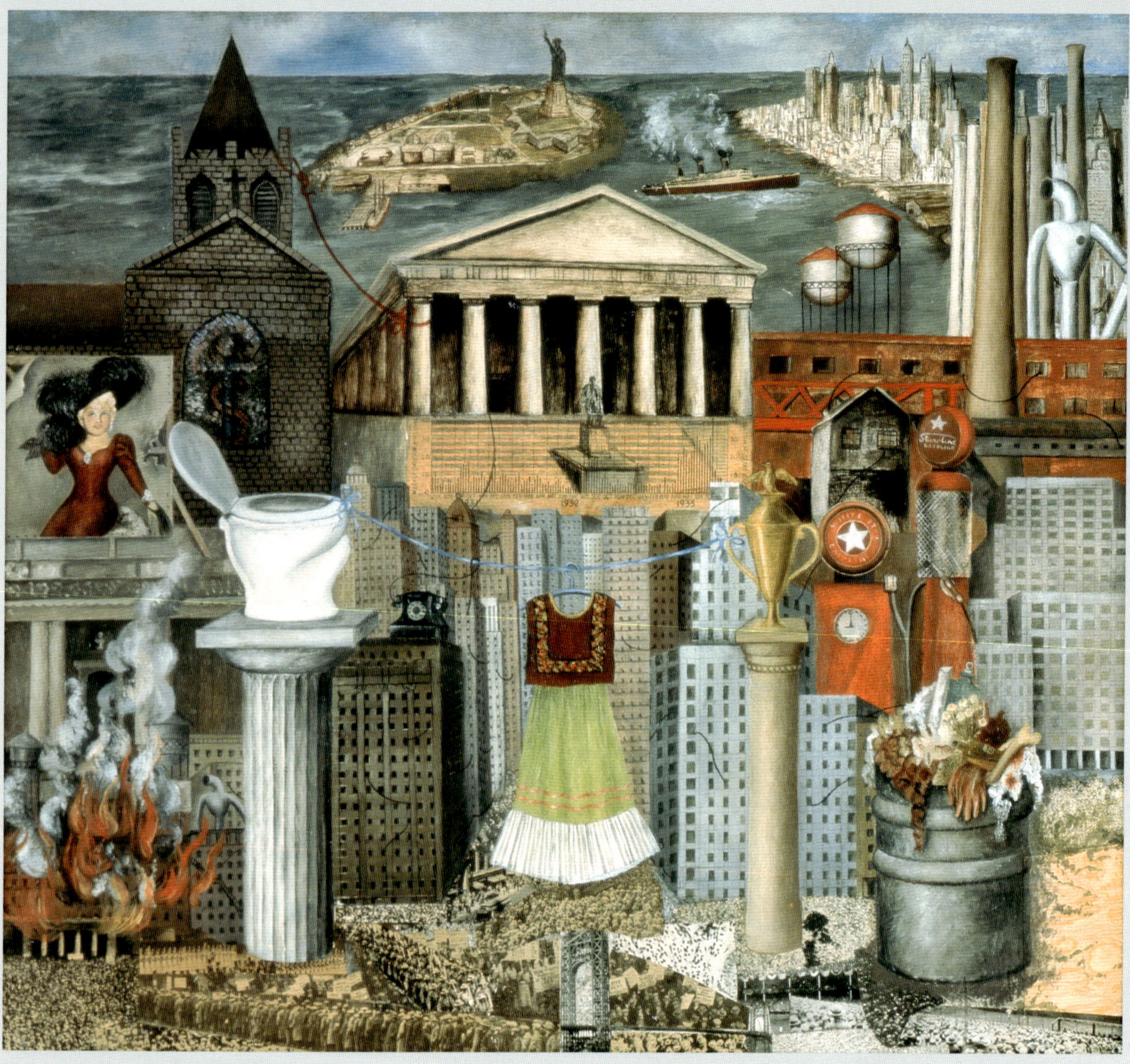

The United States

Shortly after Rivera married Kahlo, the couple traveled to the United States, staying three years. Rivera had a solo exhibition at New York's Museum of Modern Art in 1931 and mural commissions in San Francisco, Detroit, and, most famously, New York. In 1933, Rivera was invited by the Rockefeller family to paint a mural – *Man at the Crossroads* – at New York's Rockefeller Center. This project ended with the mural's destruction when Rivera depicted Vladimir Lenin among the painting's crowd of faces. While Rivera enjoyed the popularity and press attention he received living abroad, Kahlo desperately wanted to return to Mexico. A committed Marxist, Kahlo was incensed by the inequalities she observed in American society and manifested her frustrations in her painting *My Dress Hangs Here.* Against the backdrop of smoggy Manhattan, Kahlo's depiction of refuse, pollution, and prostitution conveys her disdain for American wealth and superficiality in the face of Depression-era unemployment. Indeed, the painting may be thought of as a cynical response to Rivera's lucrative commission from one of New York's most elite families. Kahlo's traditional Tehuana dress hangs loosely on a clothesline in the foreground, suggesting that although her dress – and by extension, her body – was in New York, her mind and passions remained elsewhere.

▲ Frida Kahlo *My Dress Hangs Here*, 1933

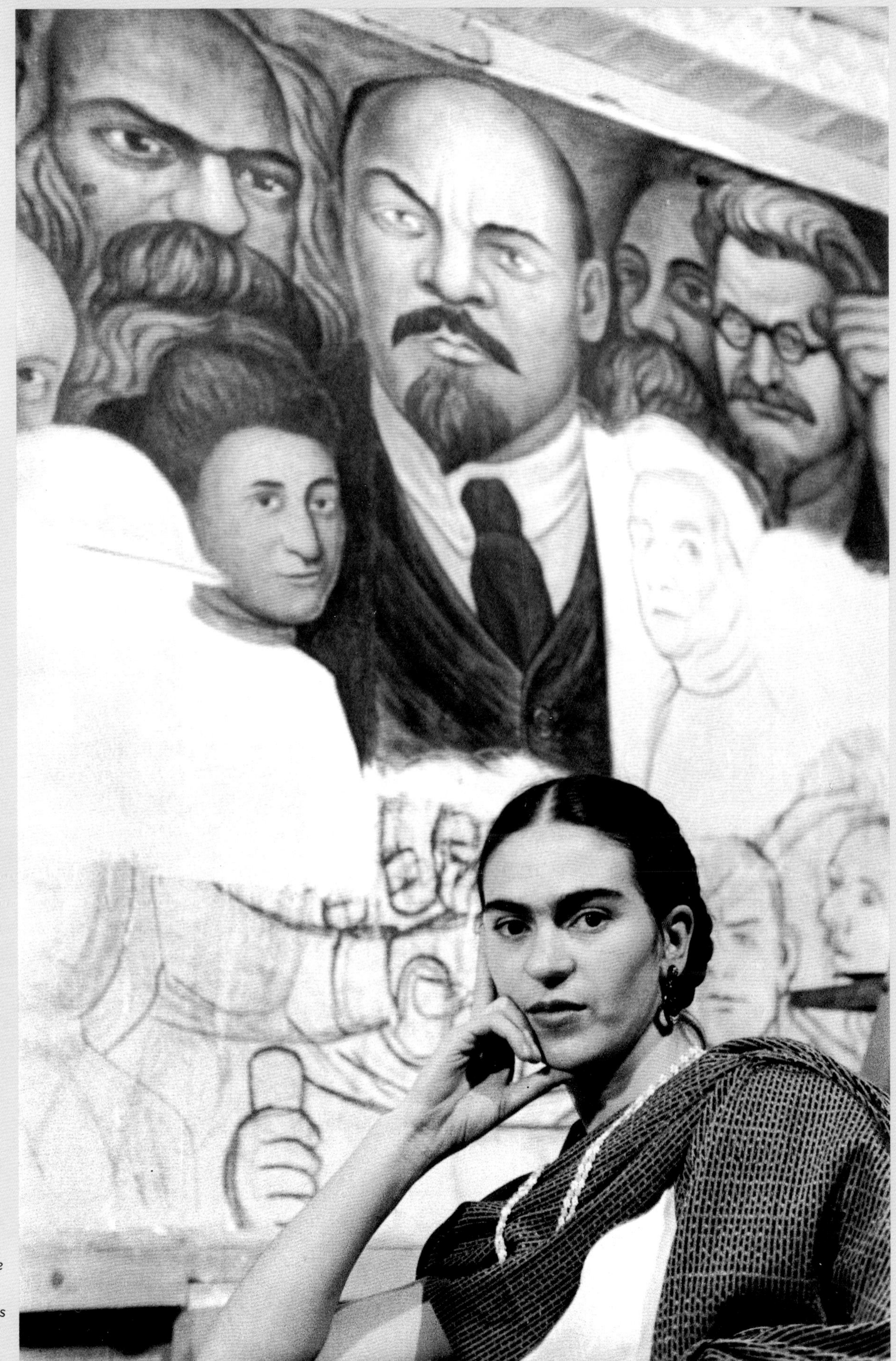

Lucienne Bloch, *Frida in Front of the Unfinished Unity Panel, New Workers School, New York City*, 1933

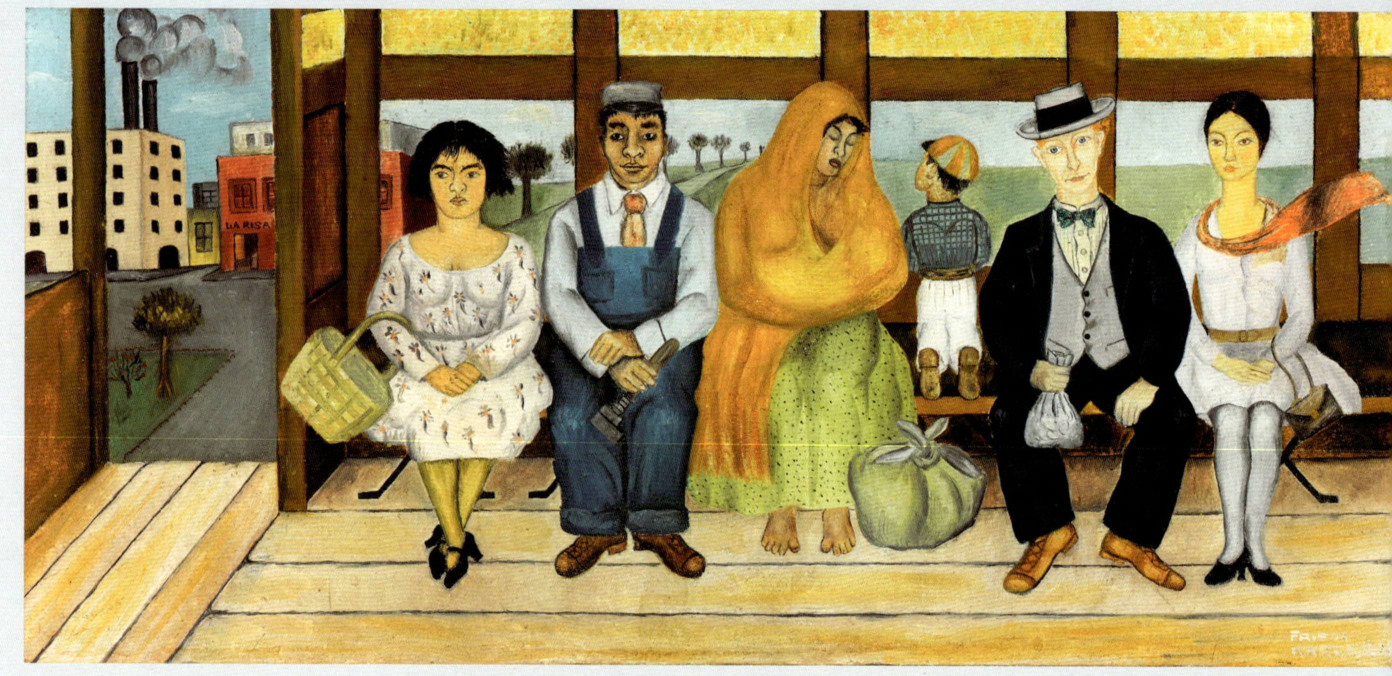

The Accident

On September 17, 1925, at the age of eighteen, Frida Kahlo was involved in a tragic accident that would change the course of her life. She and her boyfriend, Alejandro Gómez Arias, had boarded a bus in Mexico City to take them home to the suburb of Coyoacán. The driver tried unsuccessfully to pass in front of a turning trolley and collided with the oncoming vehicle. Arias miraculously escaped unharmed, but Kahlo's spine was broken in three places; she also suffered two broken ribs, a broken pelvis, a broken collarbone, and multiple fractures to her right leg and foot. An iron handrail impaled her uterus – in her words, "the way a sword pierces a bull." Kahlo spent the next three months in a full body cast. While immobilized, she asked to have a mirror hung over her bed so she could paint her reflection. In the years to come, self-portraits – some of which explicitly depict her physical suffering – would dominate her work as she underwent at least thirty-five operations on her back and legs.

▲ Frida Kahlo *The Bus*, 1929

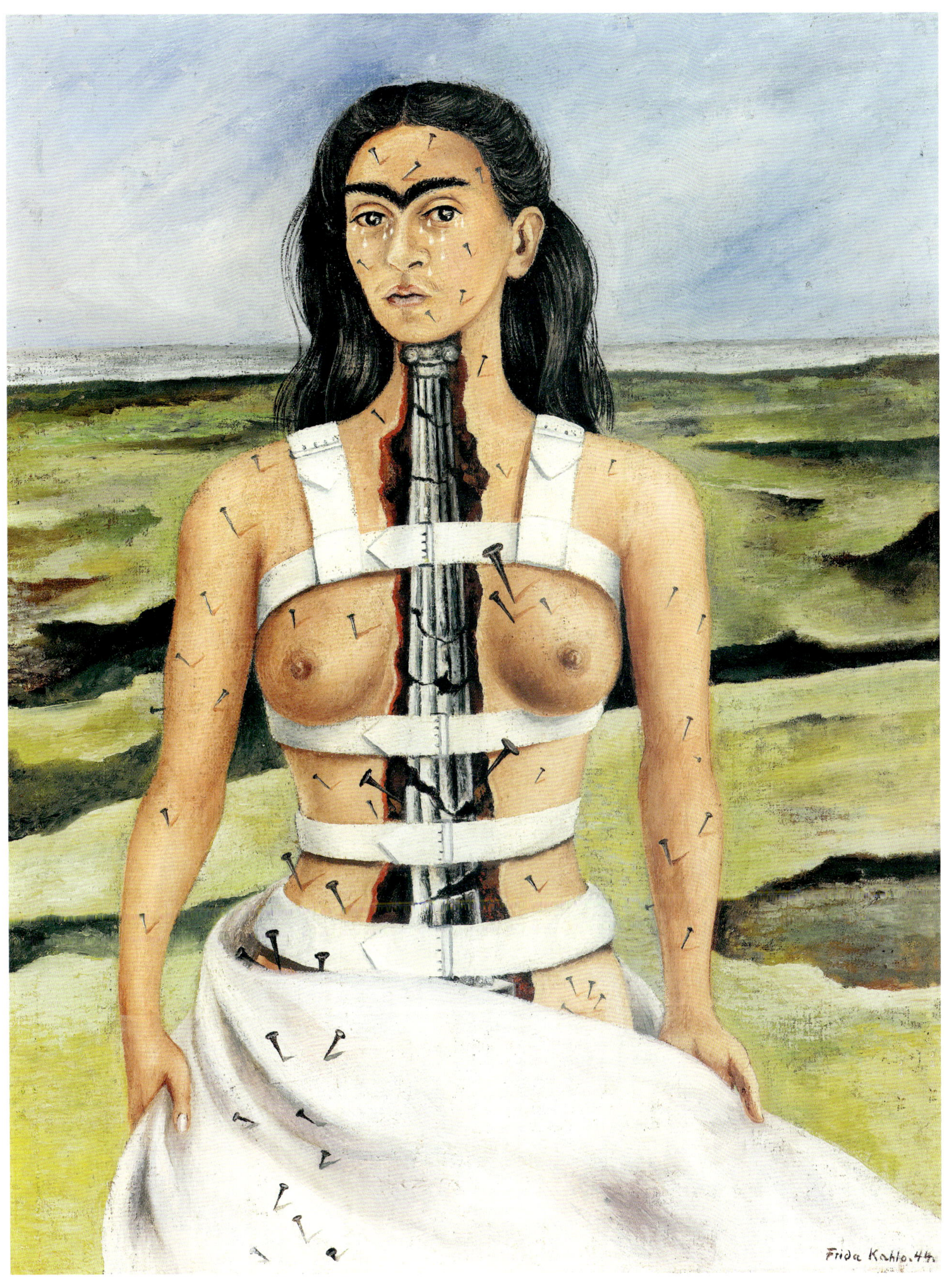

▲ Frida Kahlo *The Broken Column*, 1944

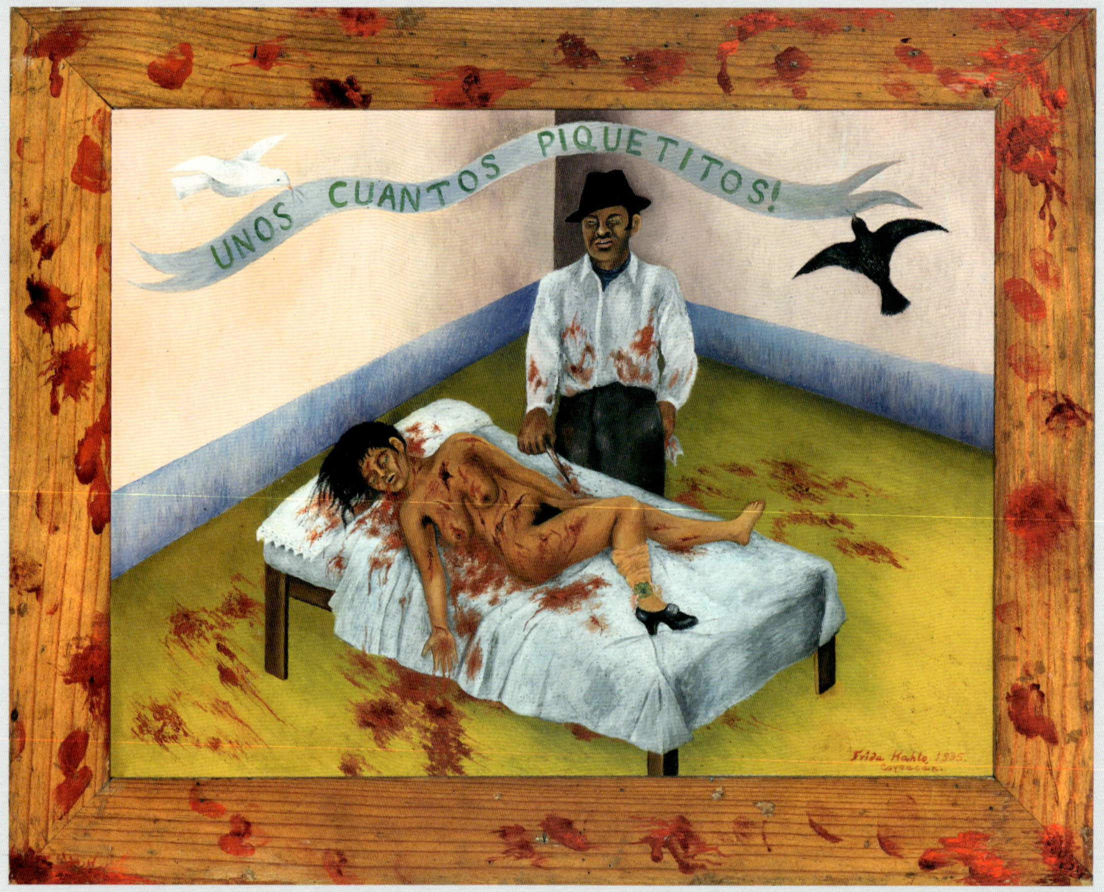

Retablos

Kahlo's distinctive style was intimately related to the popular folk art tradition of *retablos* or *ex-votos*. These small votive paintings on tin were made by anonymous artists. In *Henry Ford Hospital*, Kahlo employed the *retablo* style by placing objects in the picture relating to a tragedy – in this case, her miscarriage in Detroit in 1931. Other paintings document anguished moments in her relationship with Rivera. *A Few Small Nips*, for example, is based on an anonymous *retablo* Kahlo owned, which illustrated a woman's murder at the hands of her jealous husband; the painting may also express Kahlo's grief over Rivera's affair with her sister Cristina. *Self-Portrait with Cropped Hair* (see page 56) also invokes the *retablo* tradition, specifically in its scrolling text, a common stylistic element of this type of painting. During her life together with Rivera, Kahlo cut her hair twice: the first time after Rivera left her and moved in with Cristina, and the second time after Rivera divorced her in 1939. The inscription on the painting reads, "Look, if I loved you it was for your hair, now that you are shorn, I don't love you anymore."

▲ Frida Kahlo *A Few Small Nips*, 1935

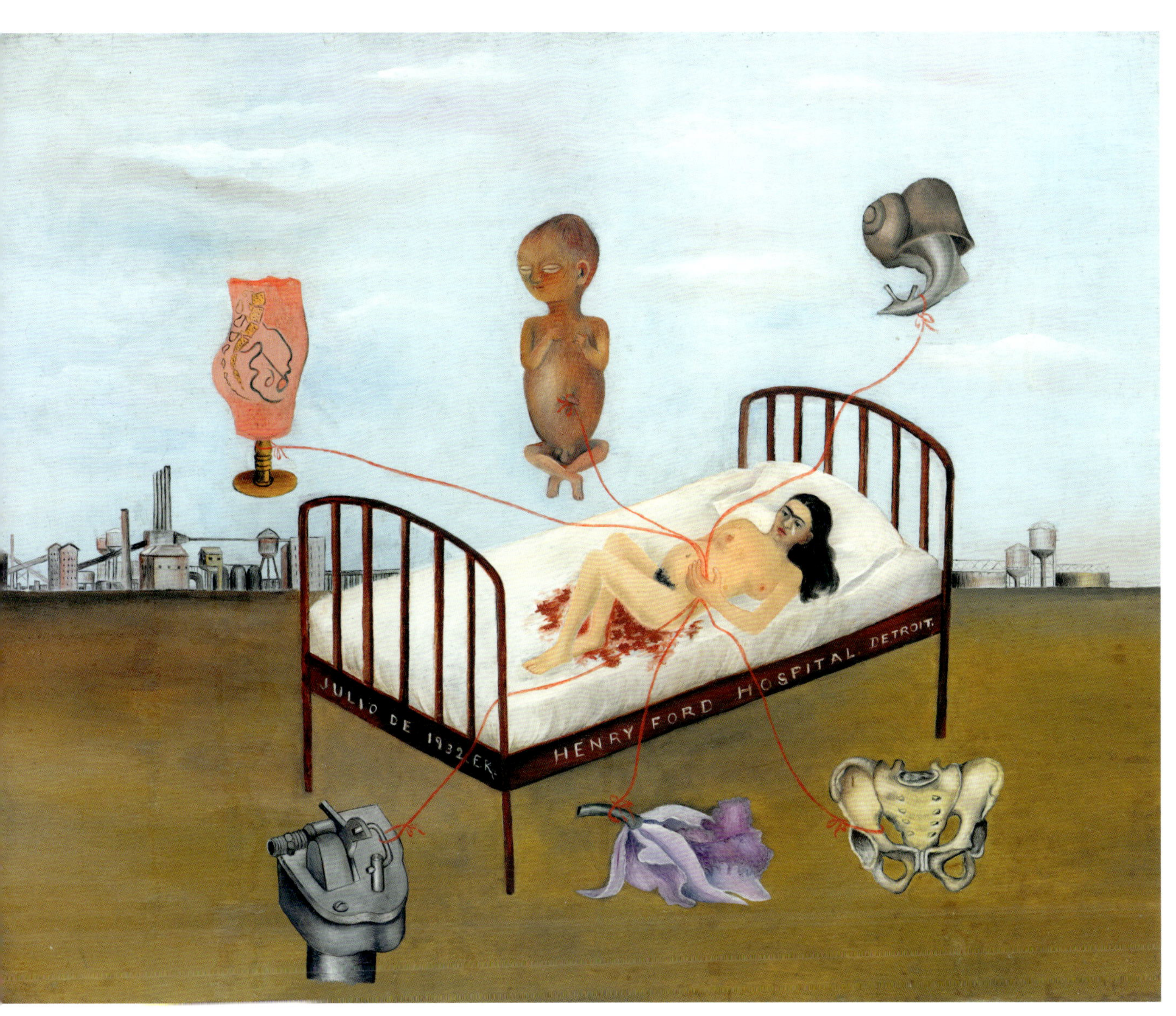

Frida Kahlo *Henry Ford Hospital*, 1932

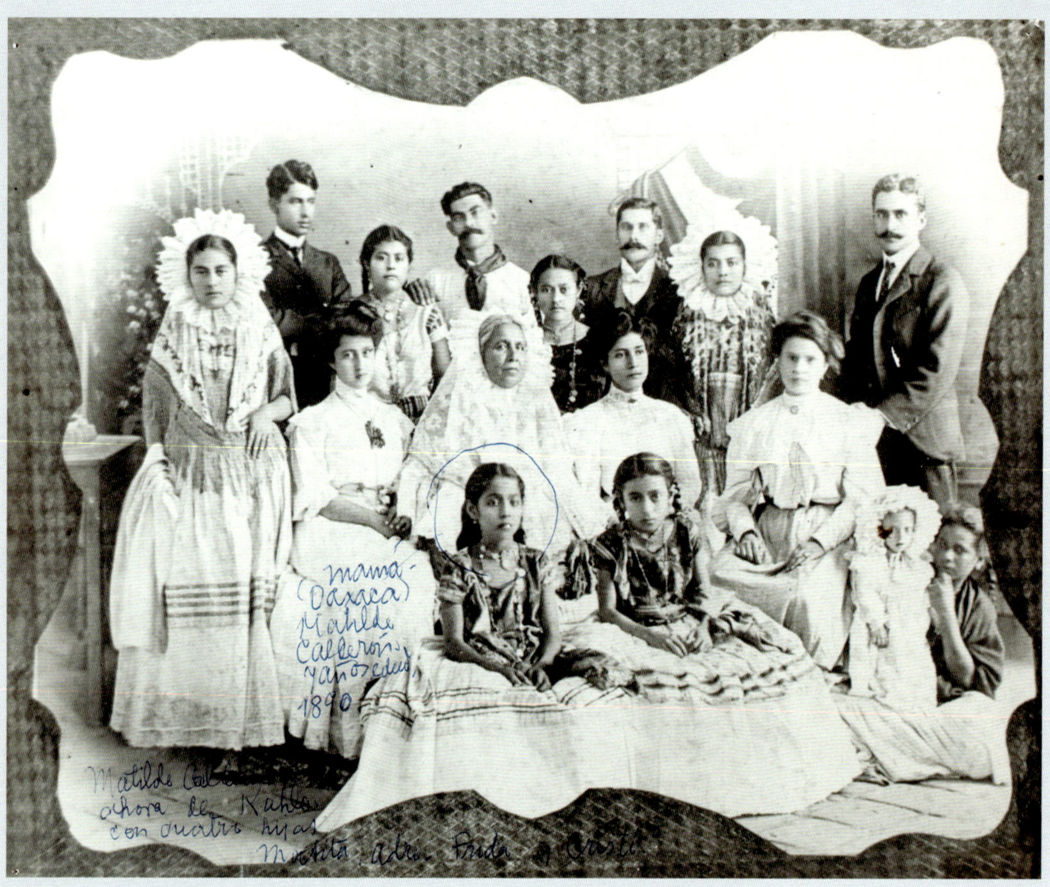

Projections of the Self

Frida Kahlo's self-portraits reflected her identity as a mestiza (of mixed European and indigenous heritage) and Mexico's rich cultural traditions through references to folk art, traditional jewelry, and indigenous clothing. Kahlo frequently depicted herself in traditional Tehuana attire—for example, *Self-Portrait as a Tehuana* (*Diego in My Thoughts*), 1943—an act of solidarity with the Zapotec women of the Isthmus of Tehuantepec, which borders the Mexican state of Oaxaca. Kahlo's mother, Matilde Calderón y González, was a mestiza from the Oaxaca region, and Rivera was entranced with the culture of Tehuantepec, which was seen by outsiders as a matriarchal society. In the post-revolutionary years, upper-middle-class women in Mexico City adopted the traditional attire of the Tehuanas to denote overt sexuality in the face of conservative social mores of demure femininity.

Kahlo's mother Matilde Calderón (circled), age 7, with her Oaxacan family, 1890

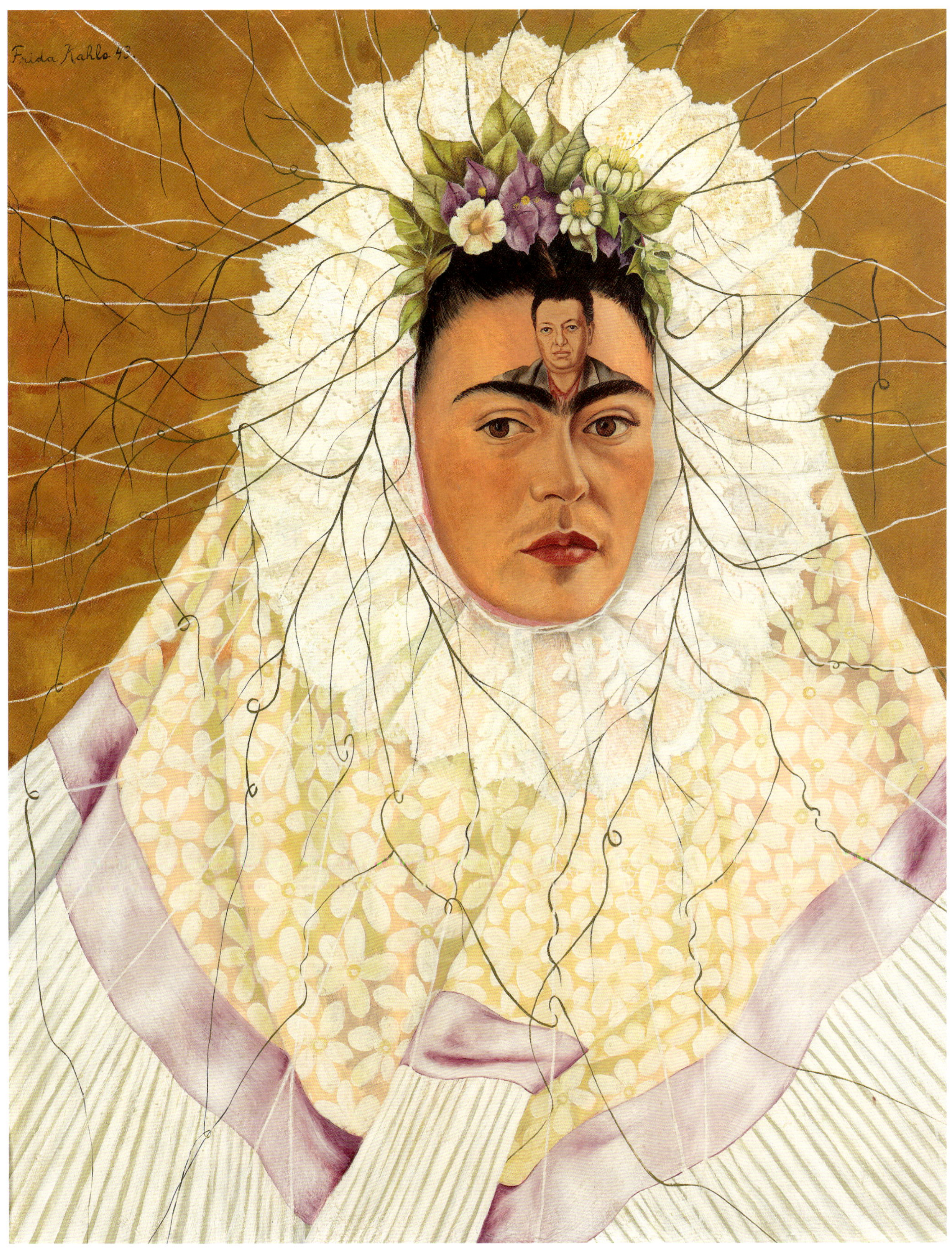

▲ Frida Kahlo *Self-Portrait as a Tehuana (Diego in My Thoughts)*, 1943

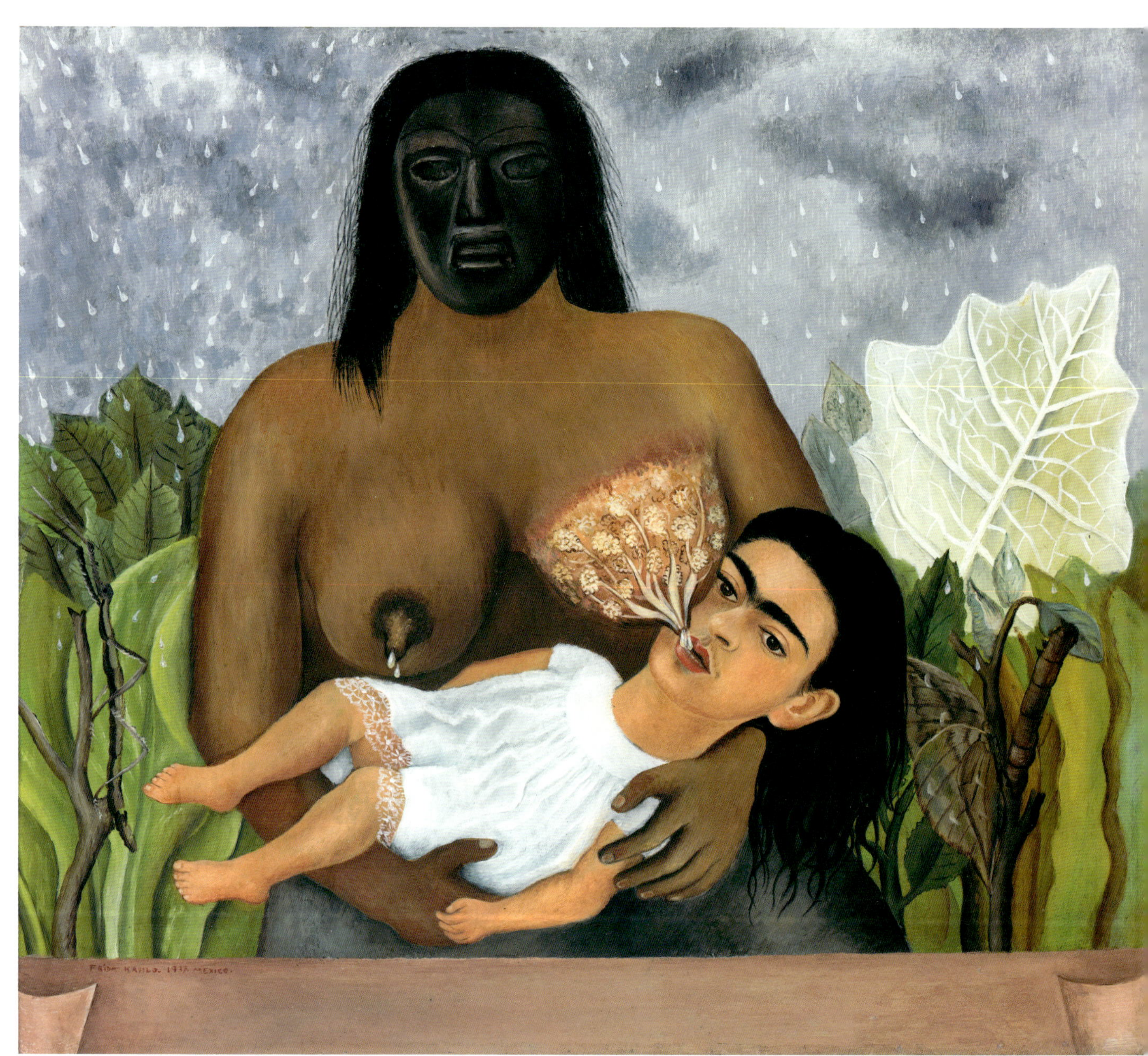

▲ Frida Kahlo *My Nurse and I*, 1937

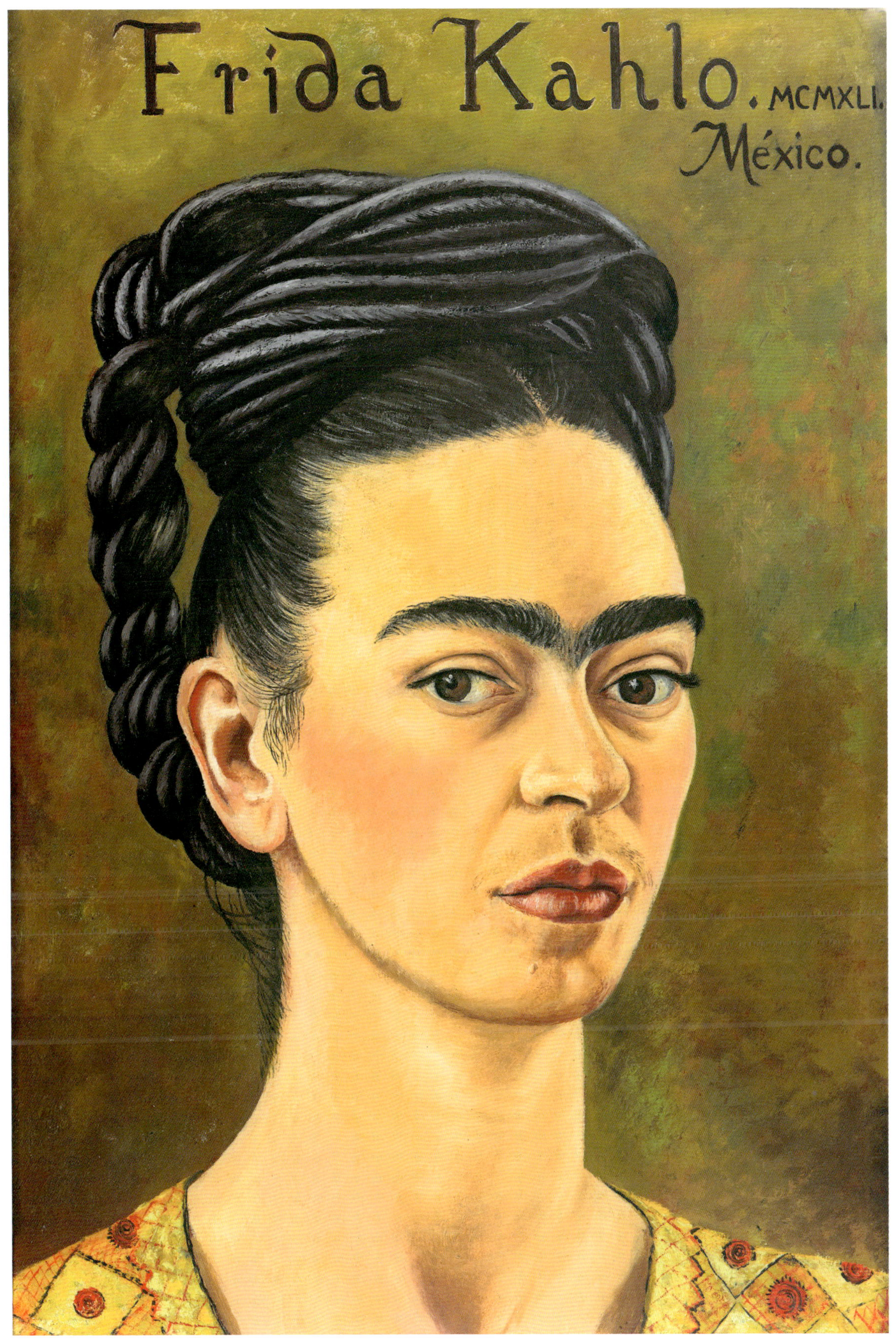

Frida Kahlo *Self-Portrait with Red and Gold Dress*, 1941

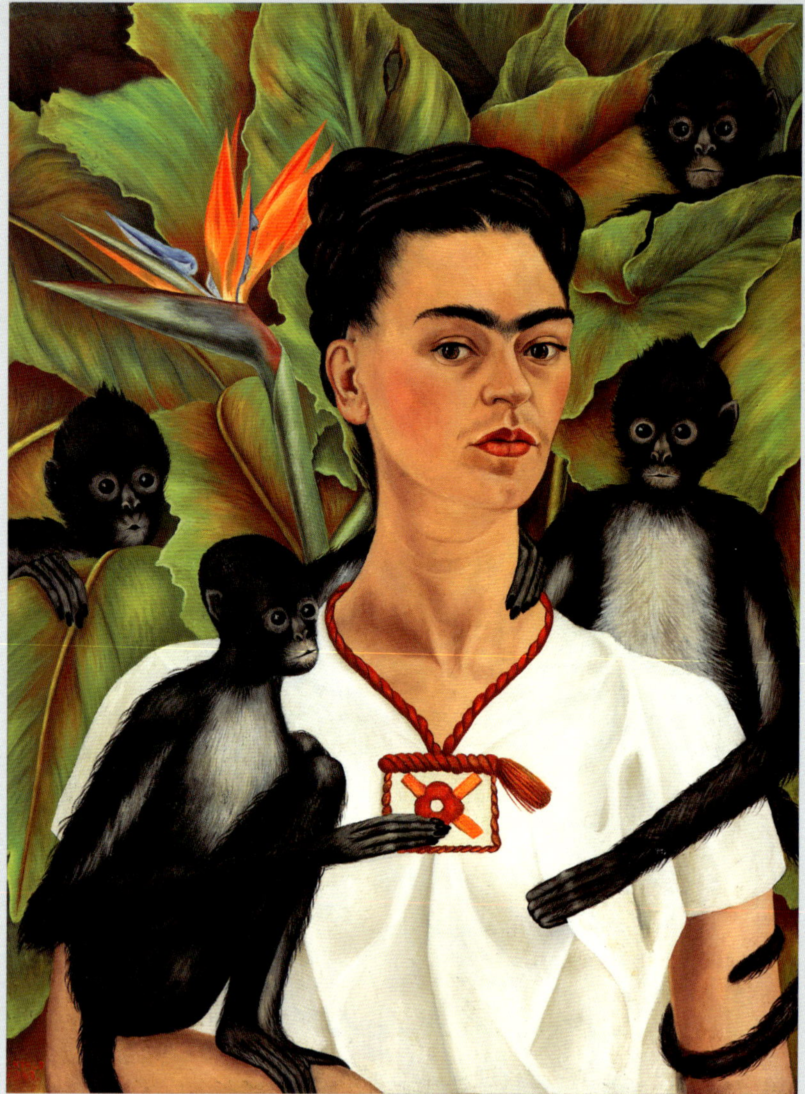

Animal Companions

Frida Kahlo owned a variety of pets that feature prominently in her paintings: her parrot Bonito; a fawn named Granizo; and an assortment of monkeys, parakeets, macaws, and sparrows. Her favourite pet spider monkey, Fulang-Chang, was a gift from Rivera and appears in a number of her self-portraits. In Mexico, monkeys are often symbols of lust, though Kahlo renders hers as gentle, protective companions. It is perhaps for this reason that scholars have frequently interpreted Kahlo's many pets as surrogates for the children she and Rivera were unable to conceive. Kahlo also owned several Mexican *Xoloitzcuintli* dogs, including one named Señor Xólotl. The *Xoloitzcuintli* are a hairless breed of dog revered by the Colima, Toltec, and Aztec civilizations. According to Aztec cosmology, the god Xólotl made the *Xoloitzcuintli* from a sliver of the Bone of Life and presented the dog as a gift to humanity. *Xoloitzcuintli* were believed to guide the dead into the underworld.

▲ Frida Kahlo *Self-Portrait with Monkeys*, 1943

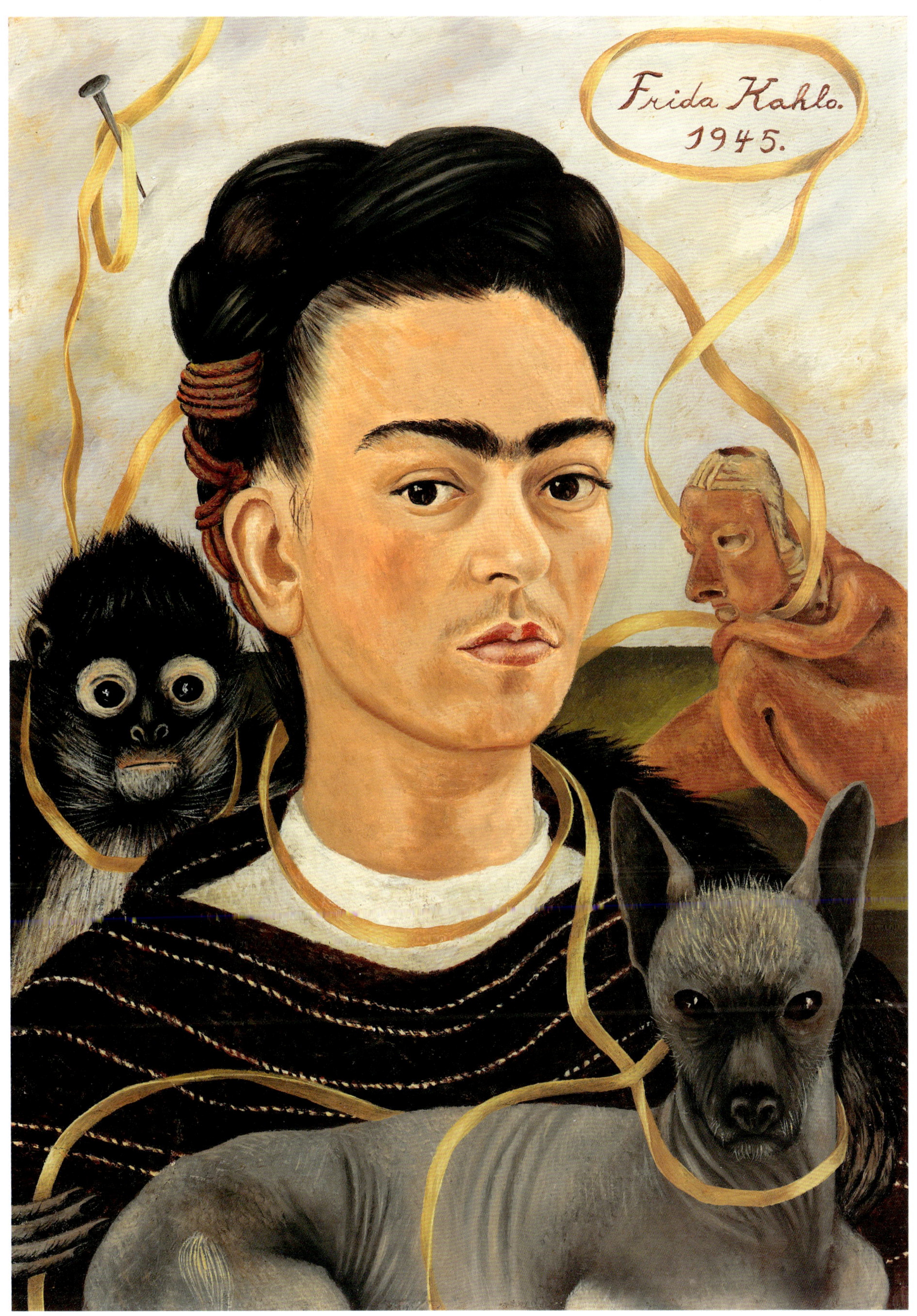

Frida Kahlo *Self-Portrait with Monkey*, 1945

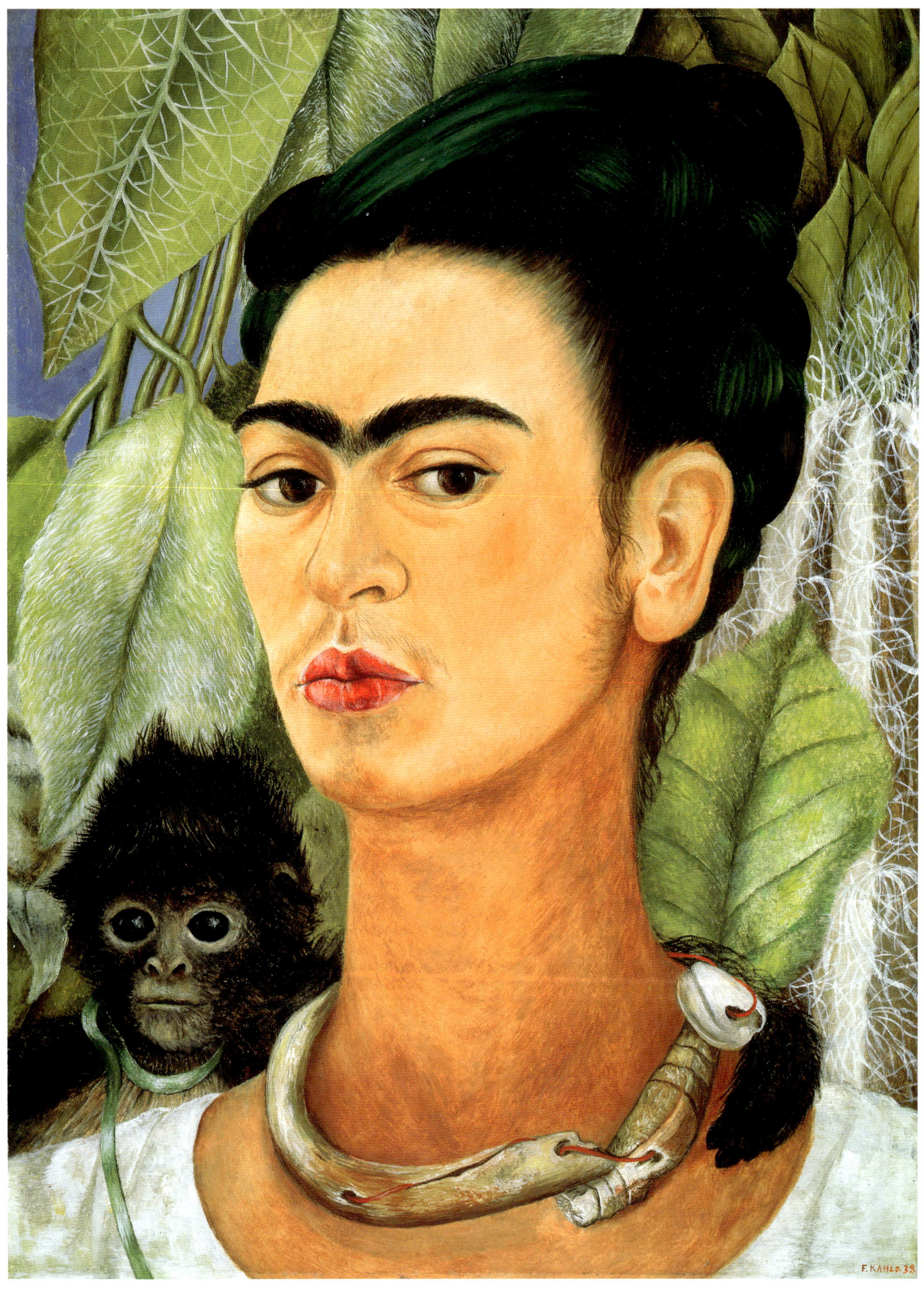

▲ Frida Kahlo *Self-Portrait with Monkey*, 1938

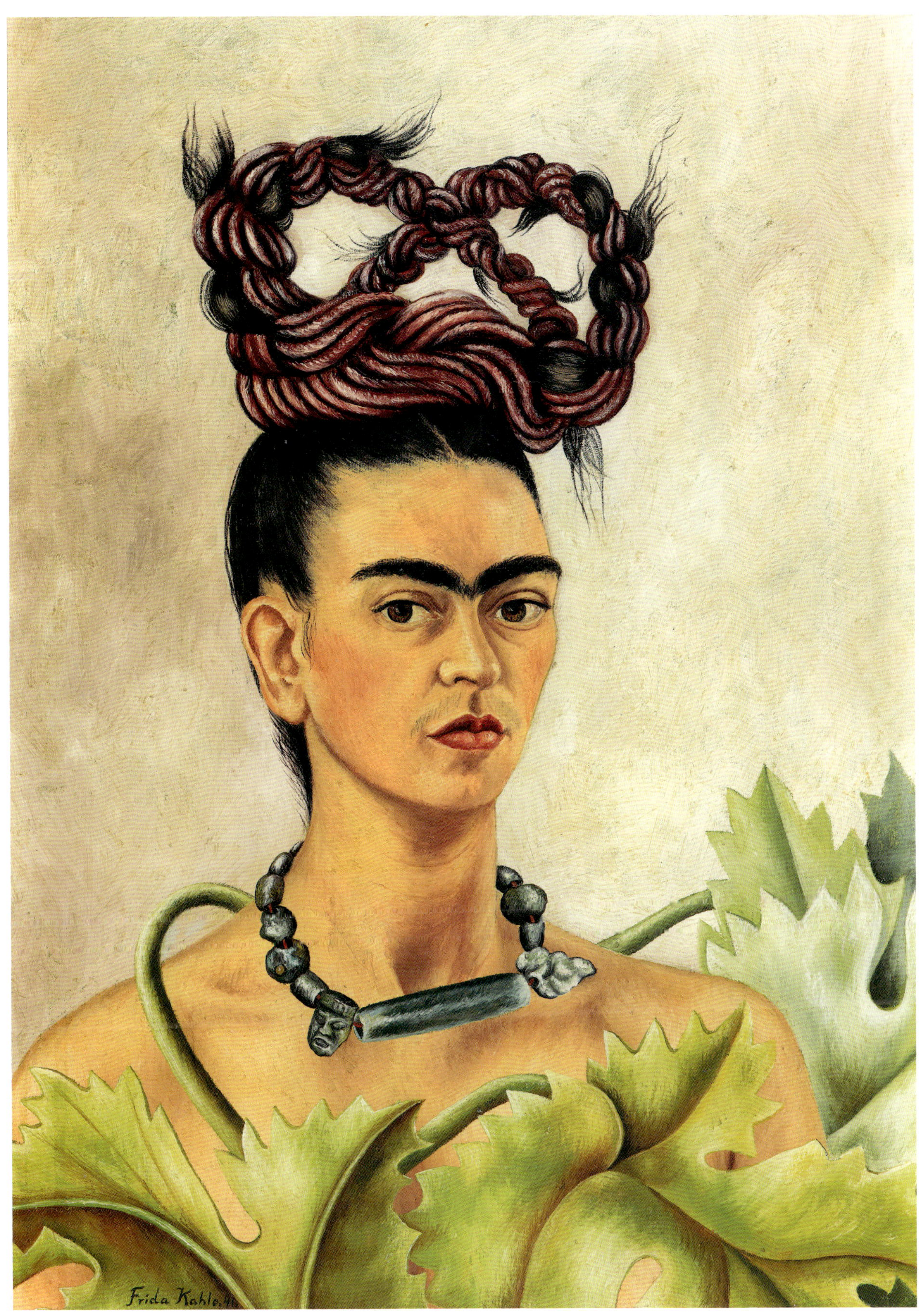

▲ Frida Kahlo *Self-Portrait with Braid*, 1941

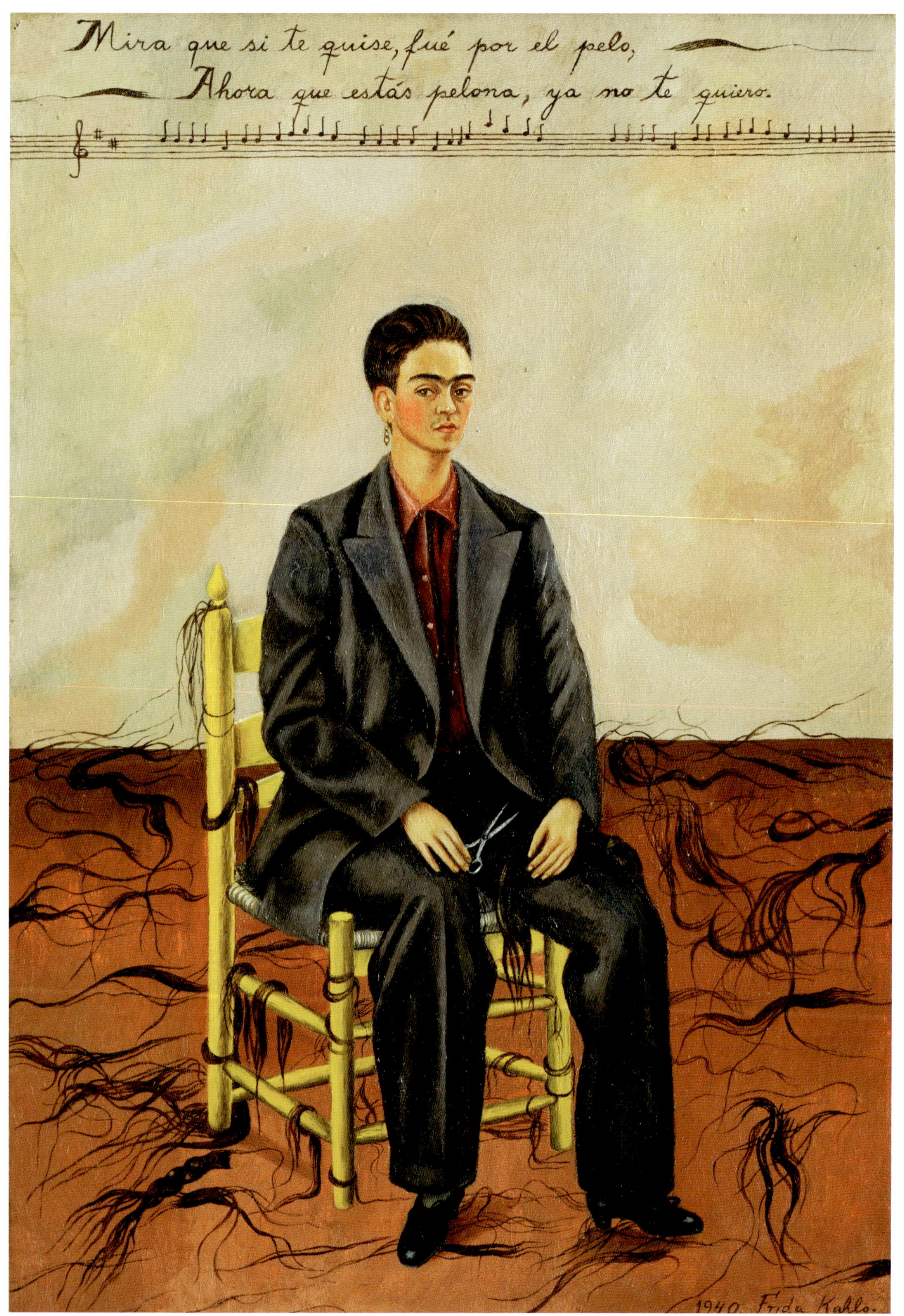

▲ Frida Kahlo *Self-Portrait with Cropped Hair*, 1940

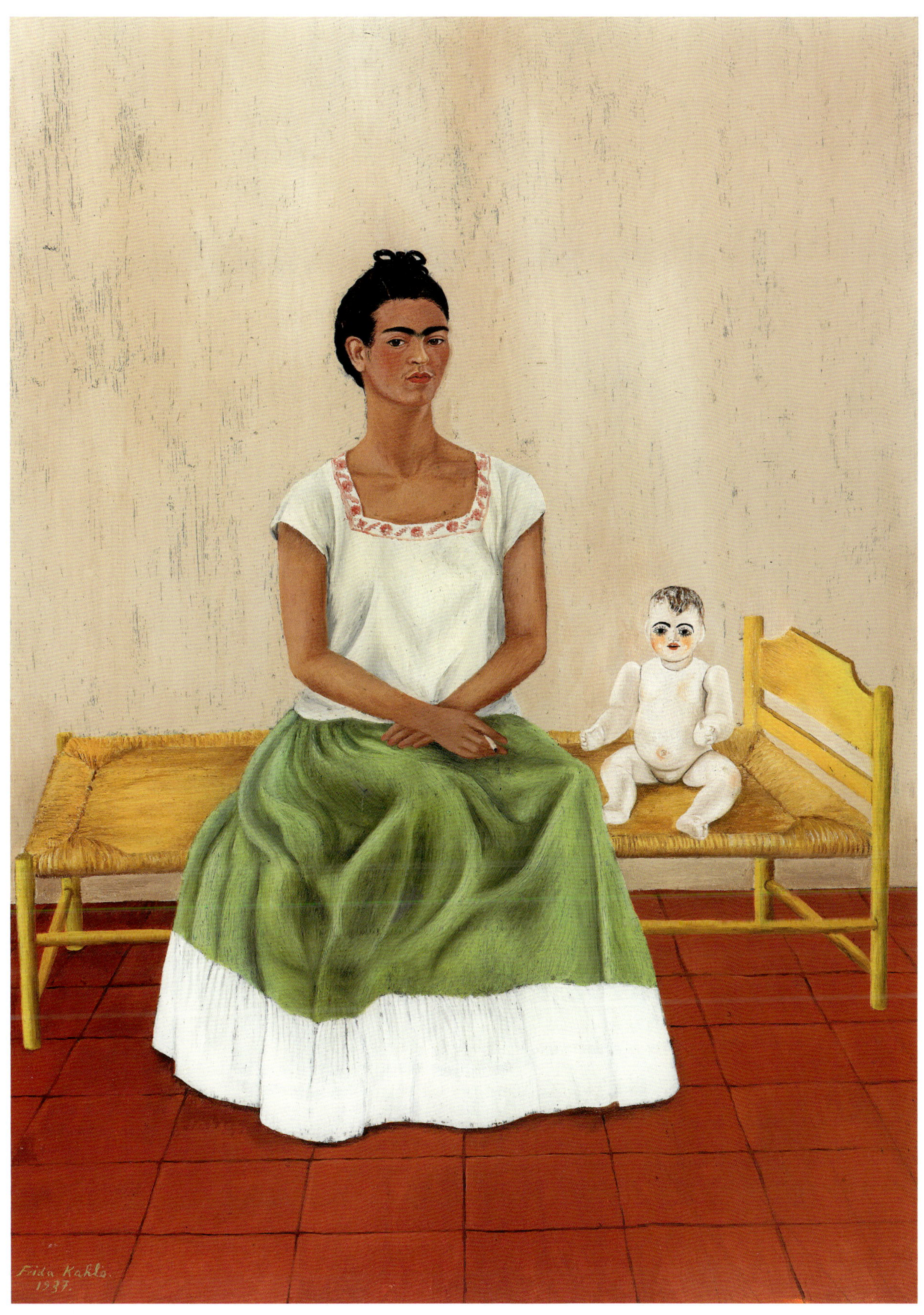

Frida Kahlo *Self-Portrait Sitting on the Bed (Me and My Doll)*, 1937

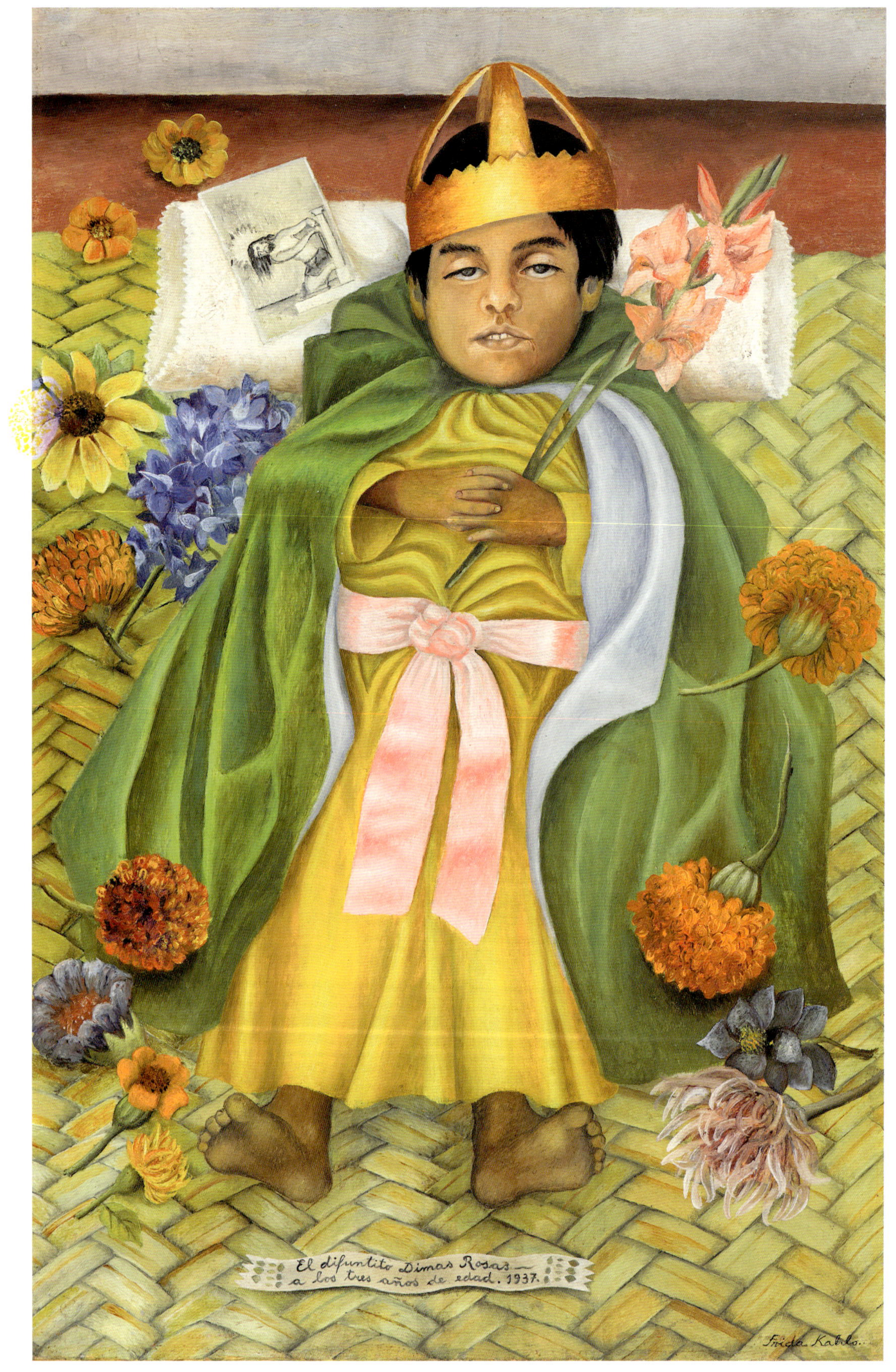

Frida Kahlo *The Deceased Dimas Rosas, Aged Three*, 1937

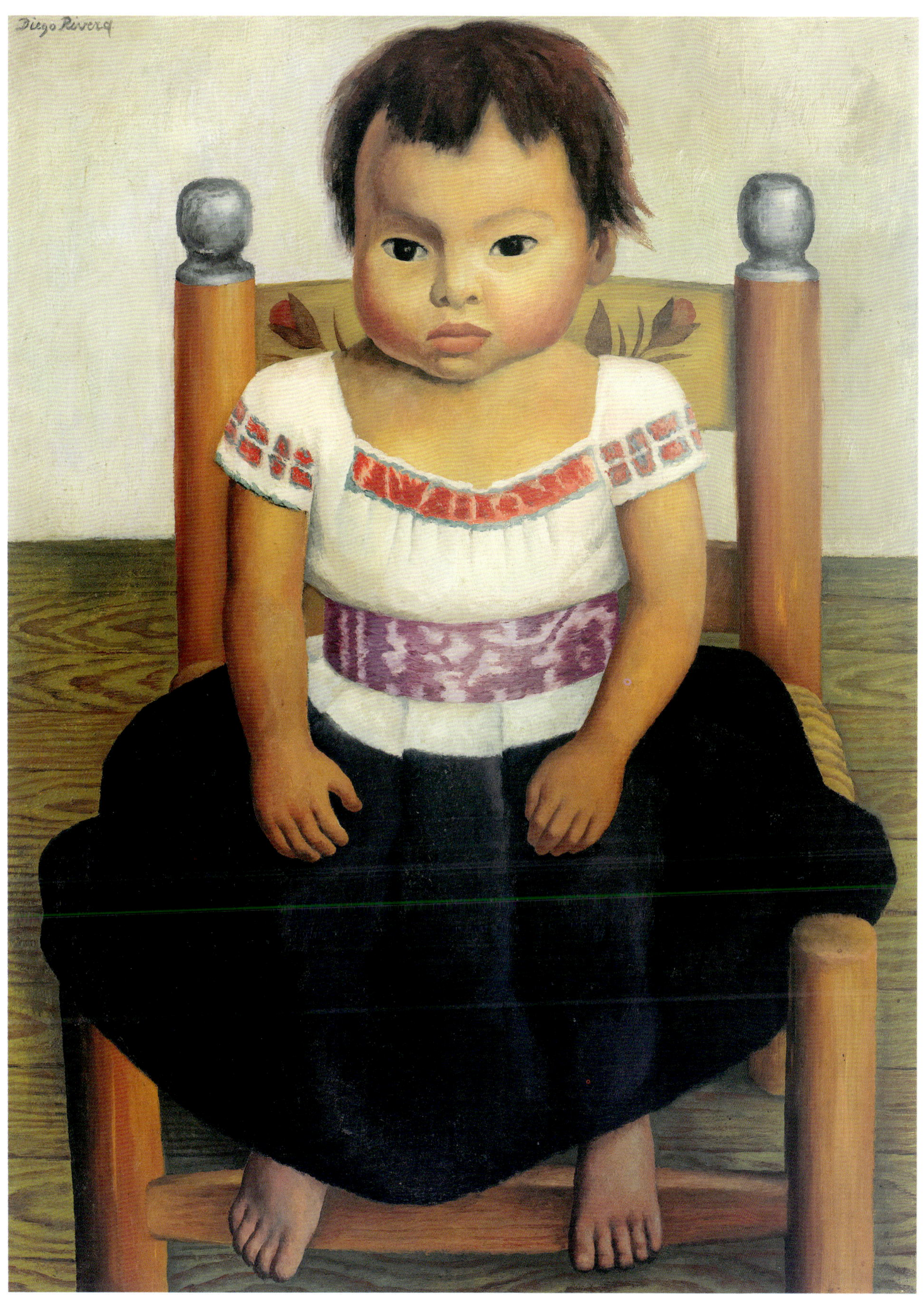

▲ Diego Rivera *Modesta*, 1937

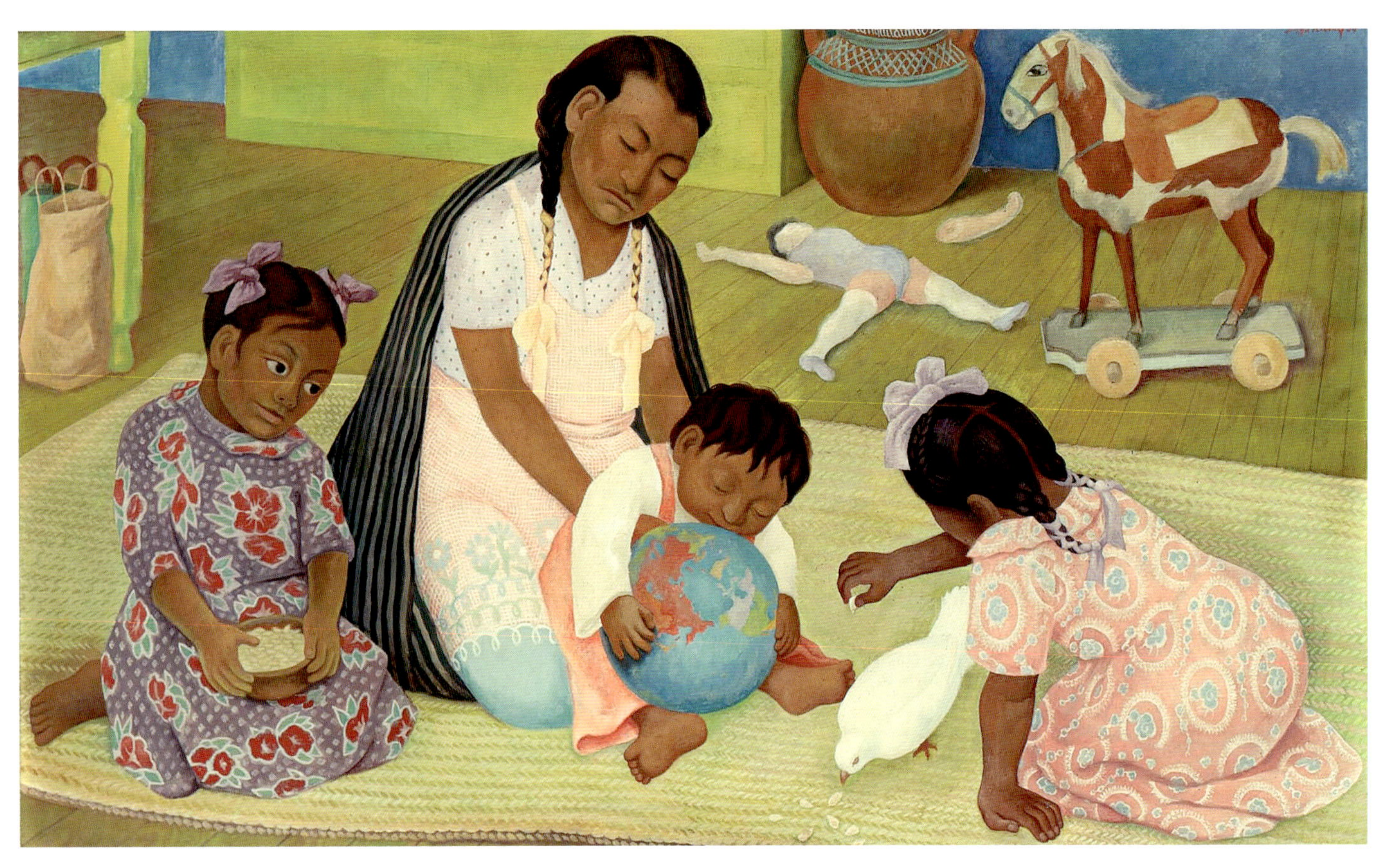

▲ Diego Rivera *Maternity*, 1954

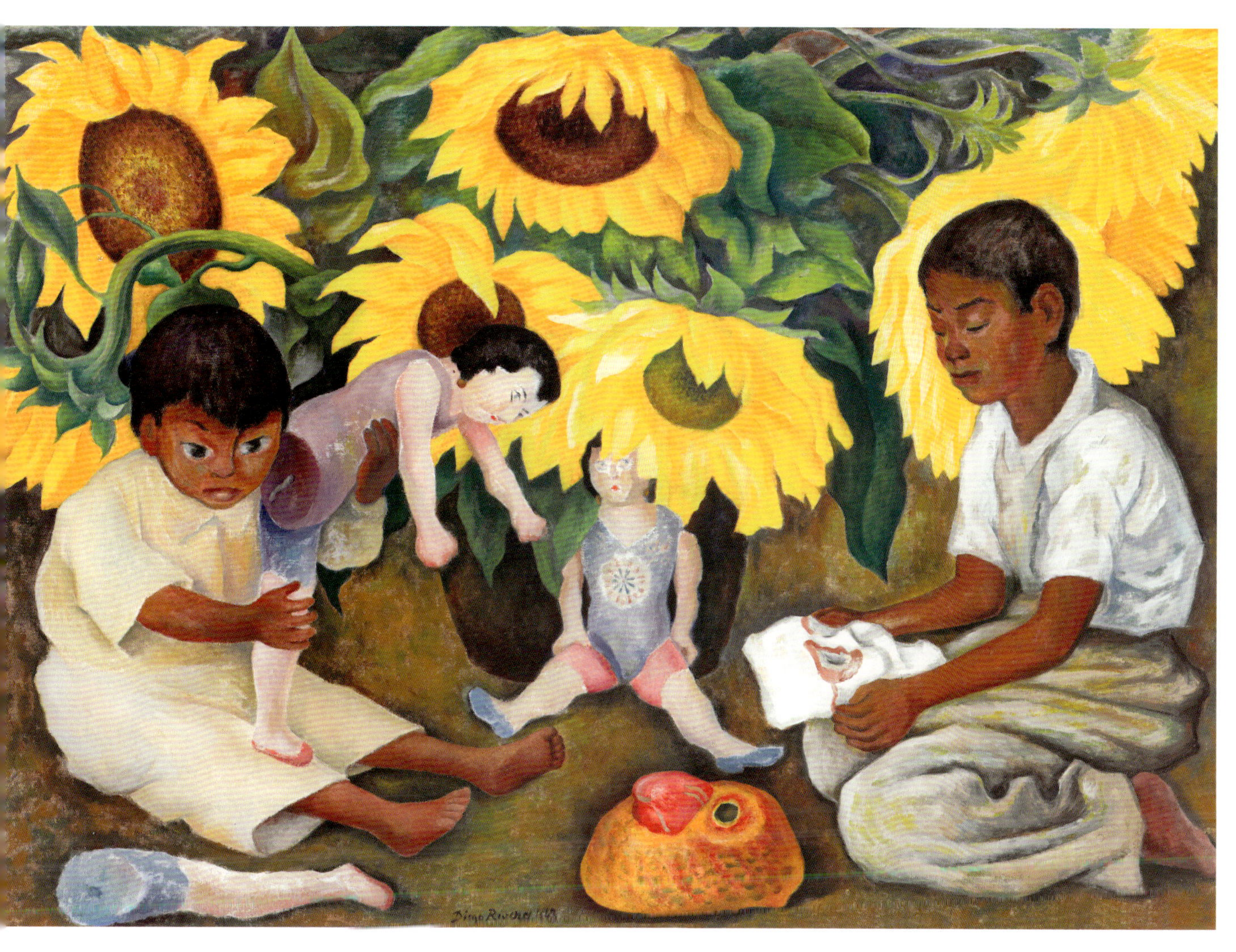

▲ Diego Rivera *Sunflowers*, 1943

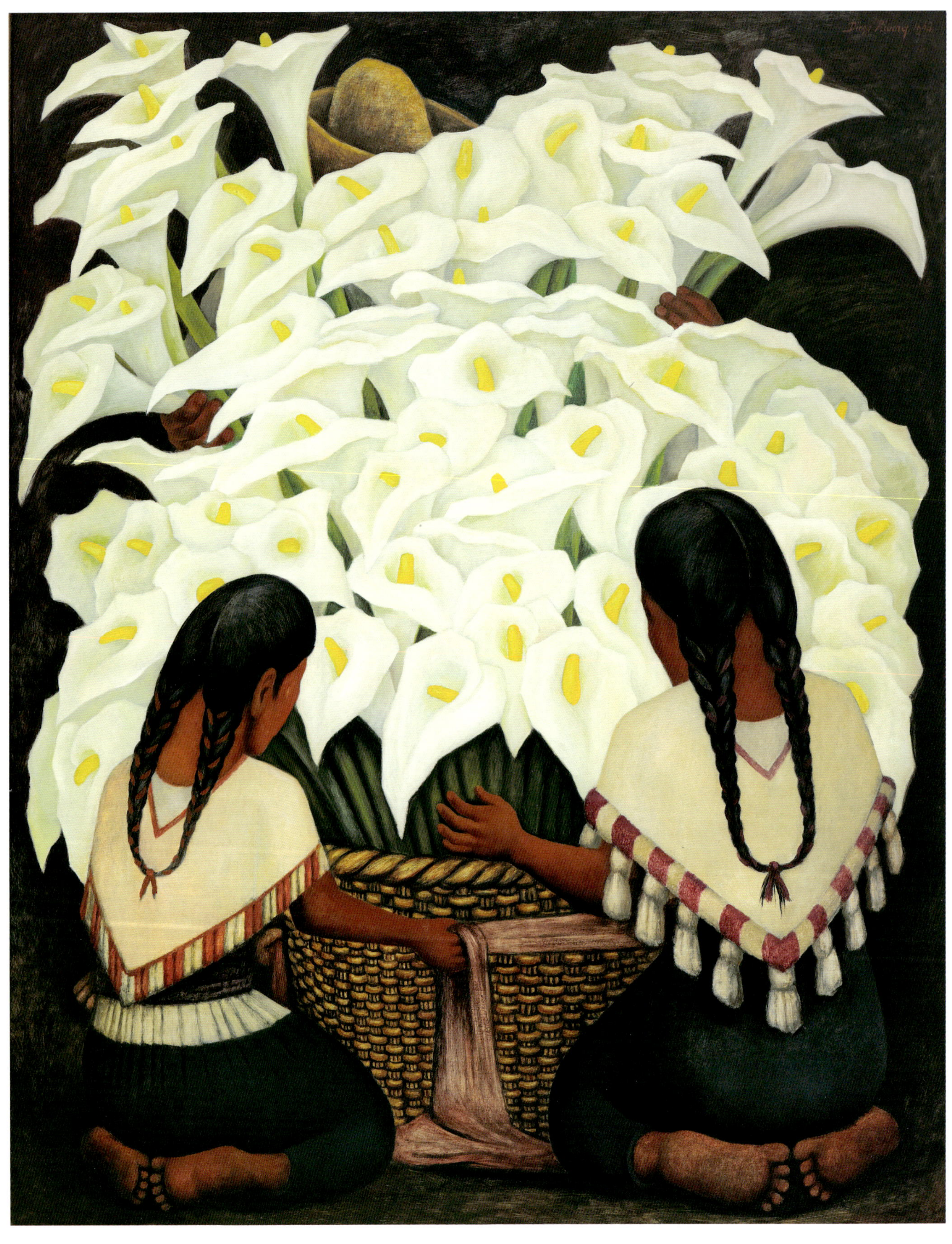

▲ Diego Rivera *Calla Lily Vendor*, 1943

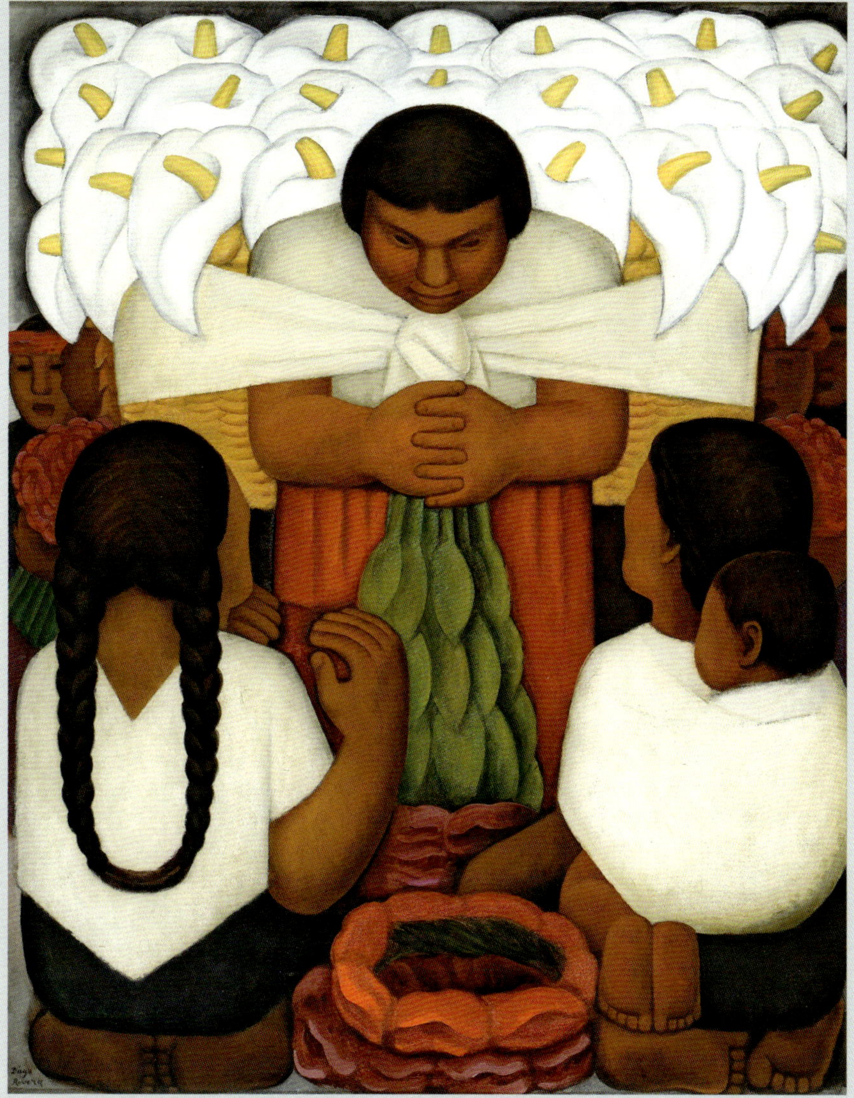

Flowers

One of the most distinctive aspects of Diego Rivera's easel paintings was the predominance of calla lilies, which reflected his fascination with the pre-conquest world of the Mexica people known as Aztecs. For the Mexica people, flowers embodied the sacred realm and the transitory nature of existence. Divinity was expressed through the poetic language of "flower-songs" – poems that were sung – and all the arts converged in the concept of a blossoming flower as the Giver of Life. Flowers were equally the purveyors of war and death. Magnificently plumed warriors engaged in Flower Wars dedicated to obtaining sacrificial victims for Aztec deities. The "flower songs" described how warriors fell like rain upon flowers when they died in battle. Rivera spoke of flowers in relation to his passion for Communism, telling his biographer Bertram Wolfe that he envisioned a new dawn for the Mexican people in which a red, five-pointed star in the sky would herald the future "of loving the sun and the flowers again. . . . even though for that a new Flowery War might be needed."

▲ Diego Rivera *Flower Day*, 1925

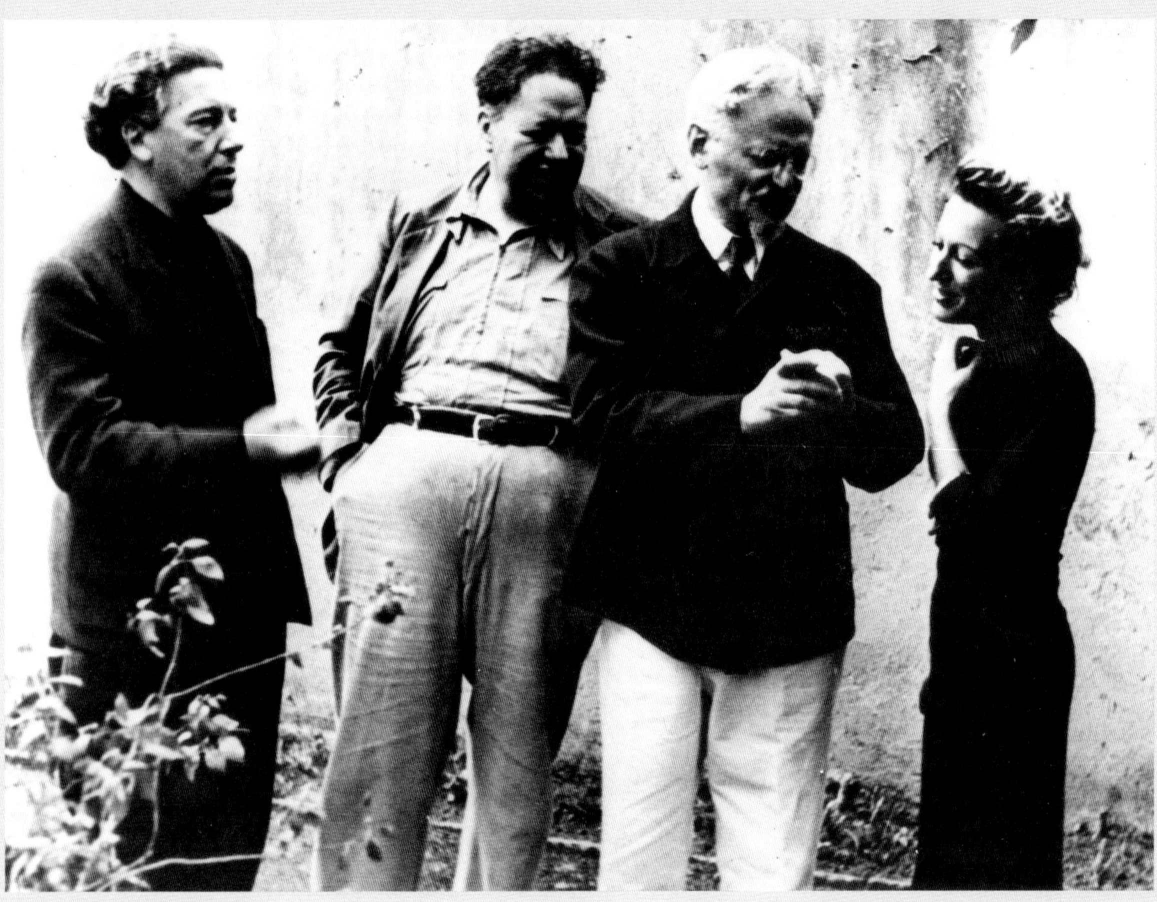

Surrealism

In 1938, André Breton, the French poet and founder of the Surrealist movement, traveled from Paris to Mexico in hopes of meeting the Communist leader Leon Trotsky, who was then in exile from Stalinist Russia and living at Kahlo's family home in Coyoacán. Breton sought Trotsky's counsel in aligning Surrealism's embrace of Freud's theory of the subconscious with Marxist revolution. Rivera, Breton, and Trotsky would write a manifesto, "For an Independent Revolutionary Art," declaring that good art was inherently revolutionary and that art should never be dictated by a political party. While in Mexico, Breton also became captivated by Kahlo's paintings, which he viewed as Surrealist glimpses into the subconscious. Describing her work as a "ribbon around a bomb," Breton arranged for Kahlo to be included in Surrealist exhibitions in Paris and New York. However, Kahlo refused to label her work Surrealist, and when she traveled to Paris in 1939 at Breton's invitation, she found the Surrealists pretentious and bourgeois. One exception was the artist Marcel Duchamp, whom she described as the only one "with his feet on the ground." Duchamp arranged for Kahlo's work to be shown in an exhibition titled *Mexique*, which resulted in the Louvre purchasing Kahlo's *Self-Portrait: The Frame* (1938) – the first work in its collection by a twentieth-century Mexican artist.

Anonymous,
André Breton, Diego Rivera, Leon Trotsky, and Jacqueline Lamba in Mexico, 1938

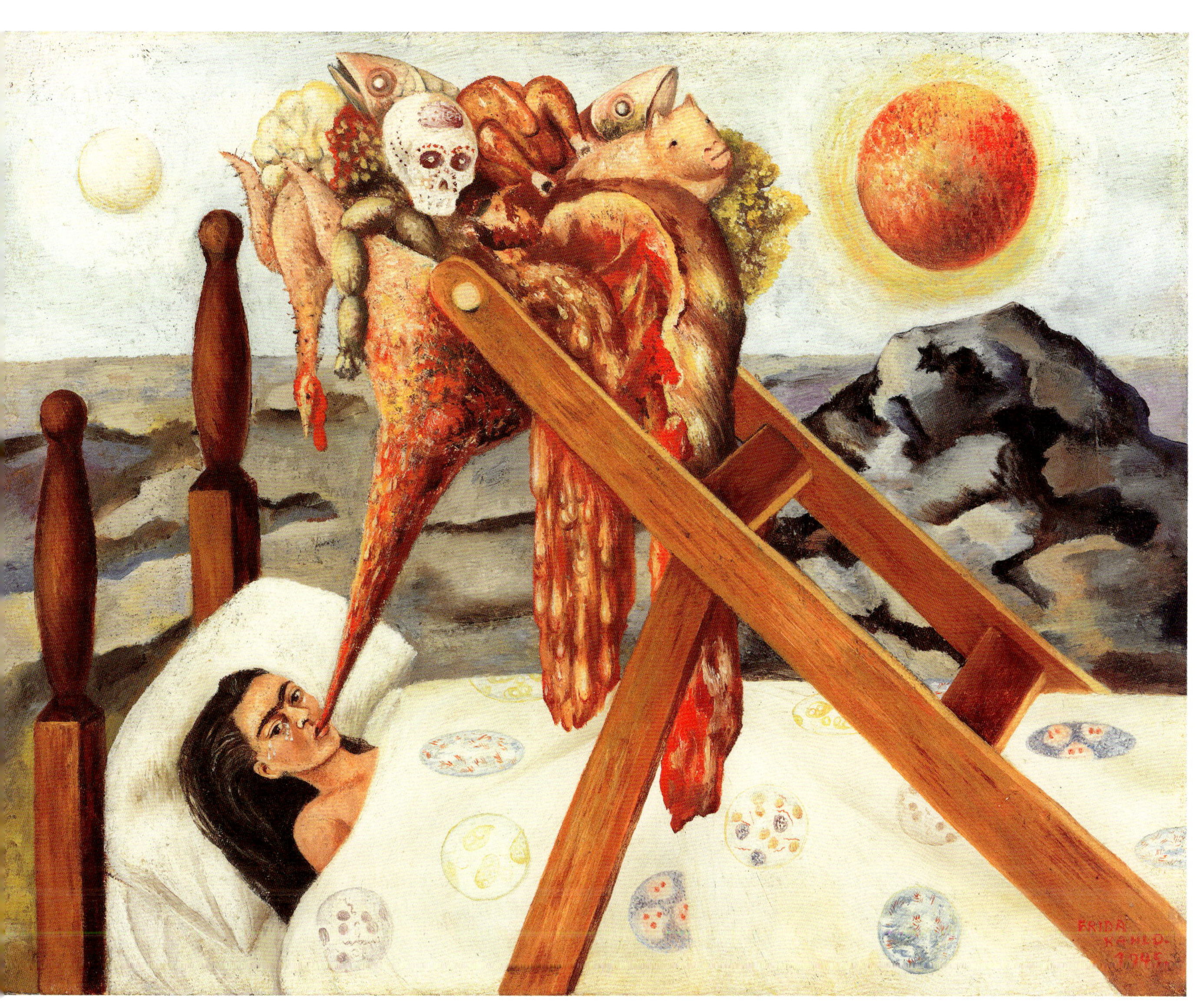

Frida Kahlo *Without Hope*, 1945

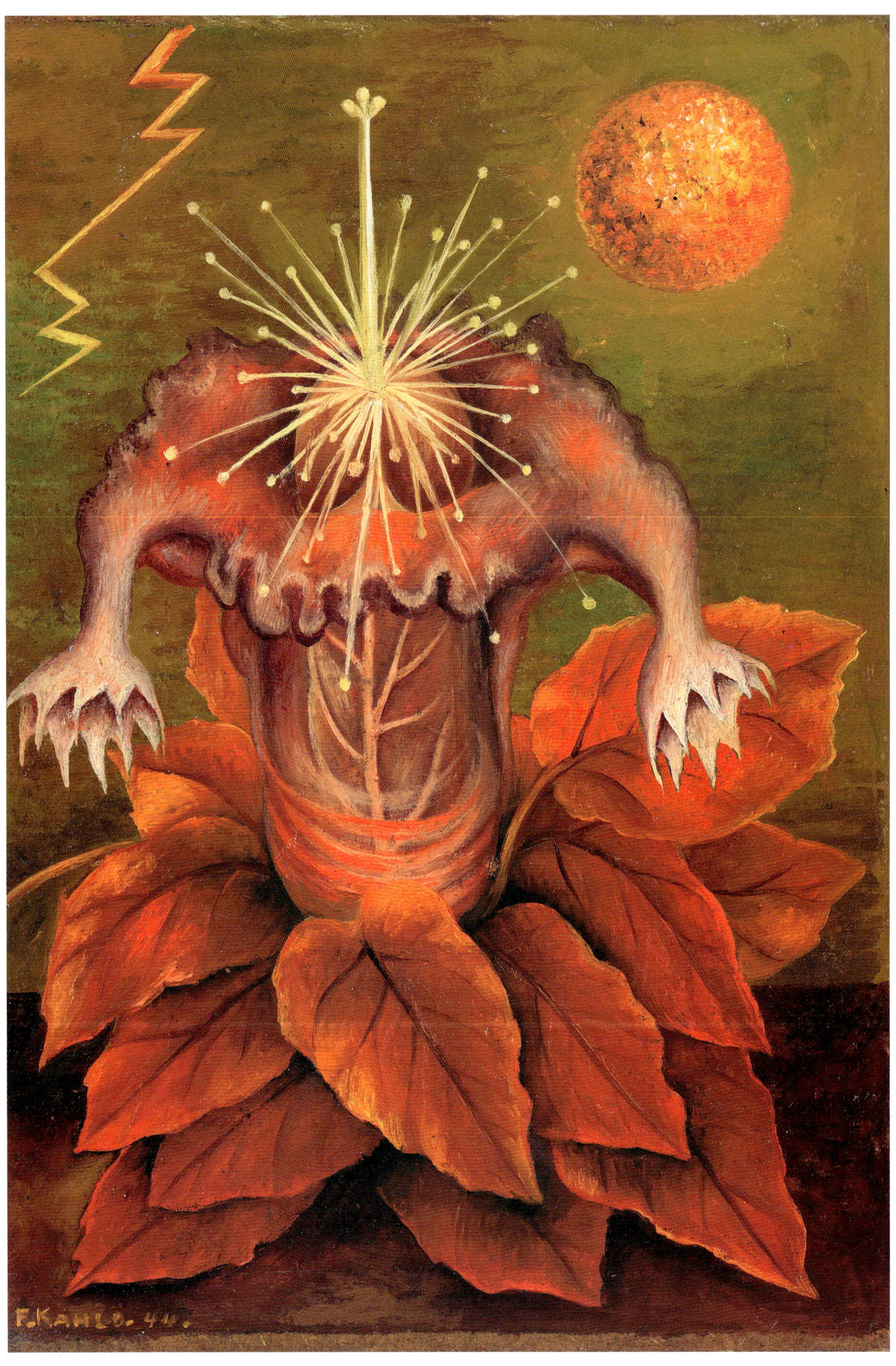

Frida Kahlo *The Flower of Life*, 1944

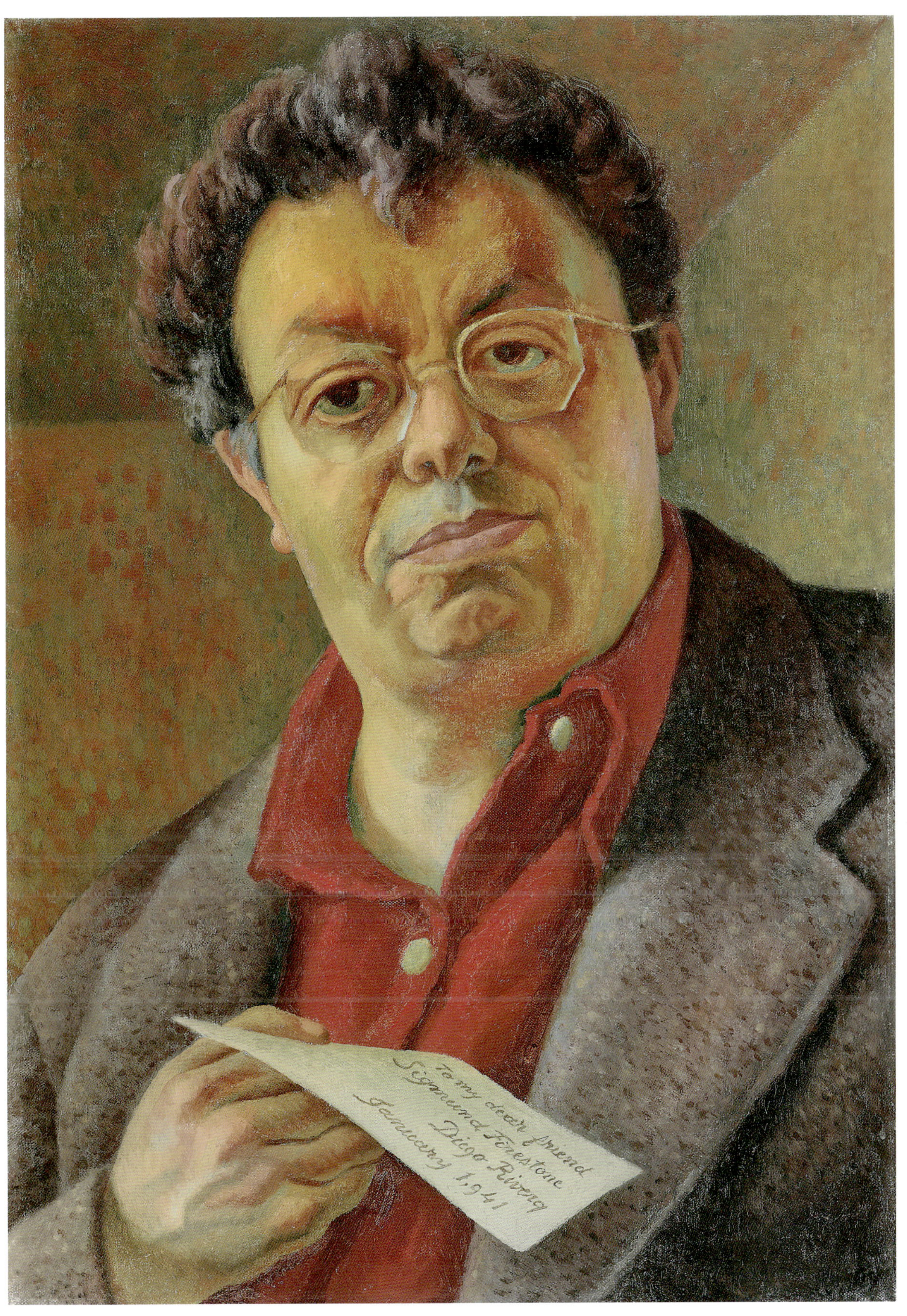

Diego Rivera *Self-Portrait*, 1941

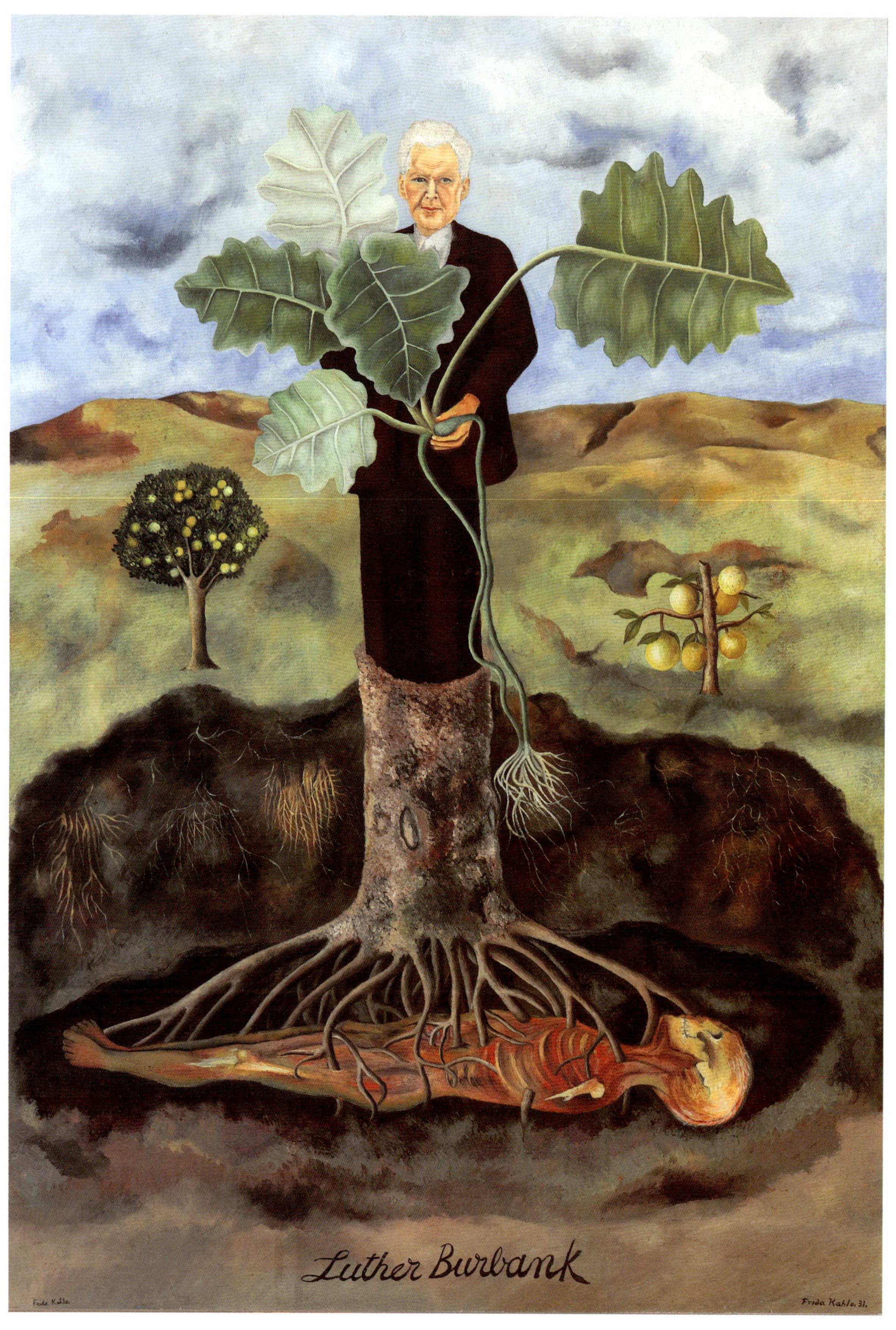

Frida Kahlo *Portrait of Luther Burbank*, 1931

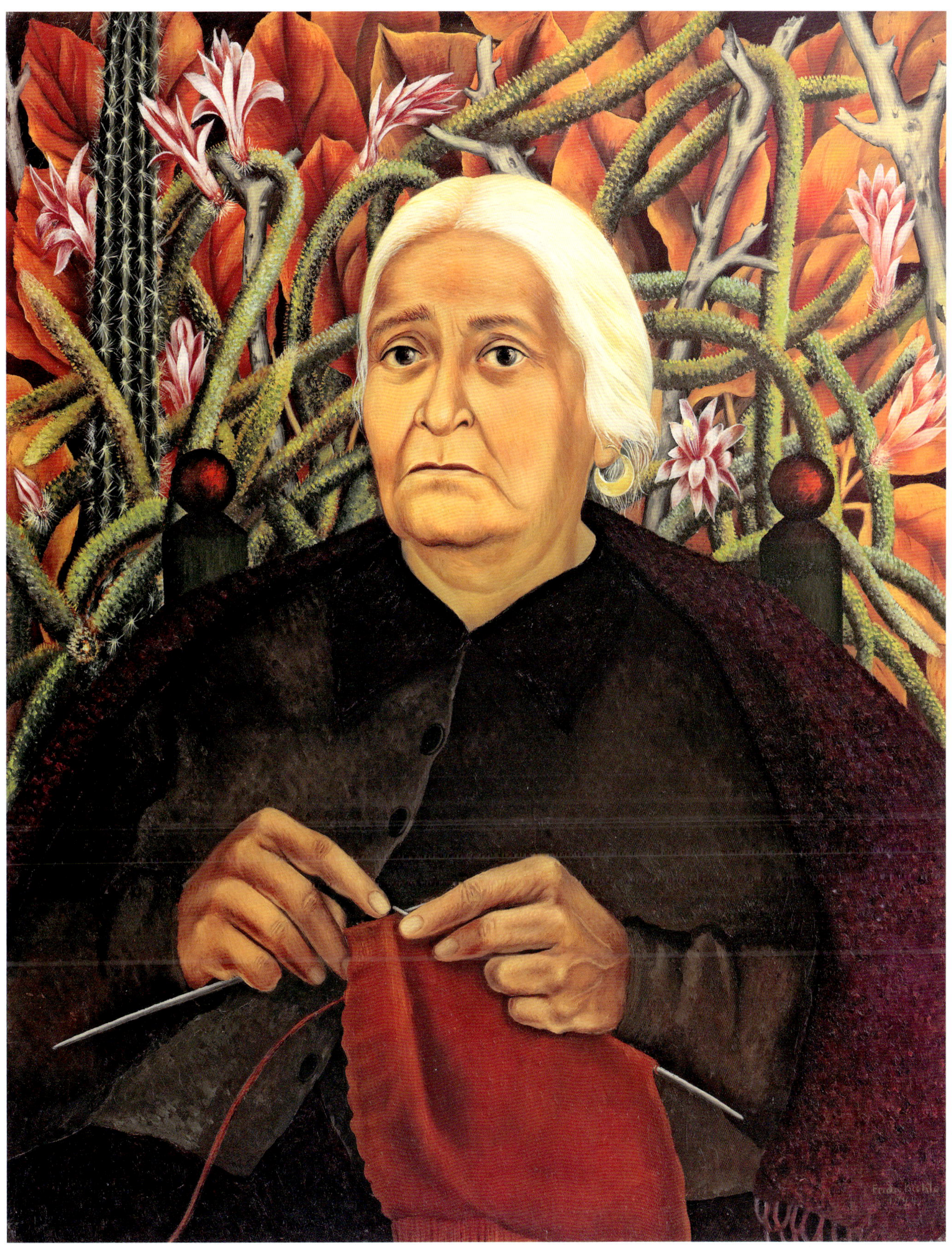

Frida Kahlo *Portrait of Doña Rosita Morillo*, 1944

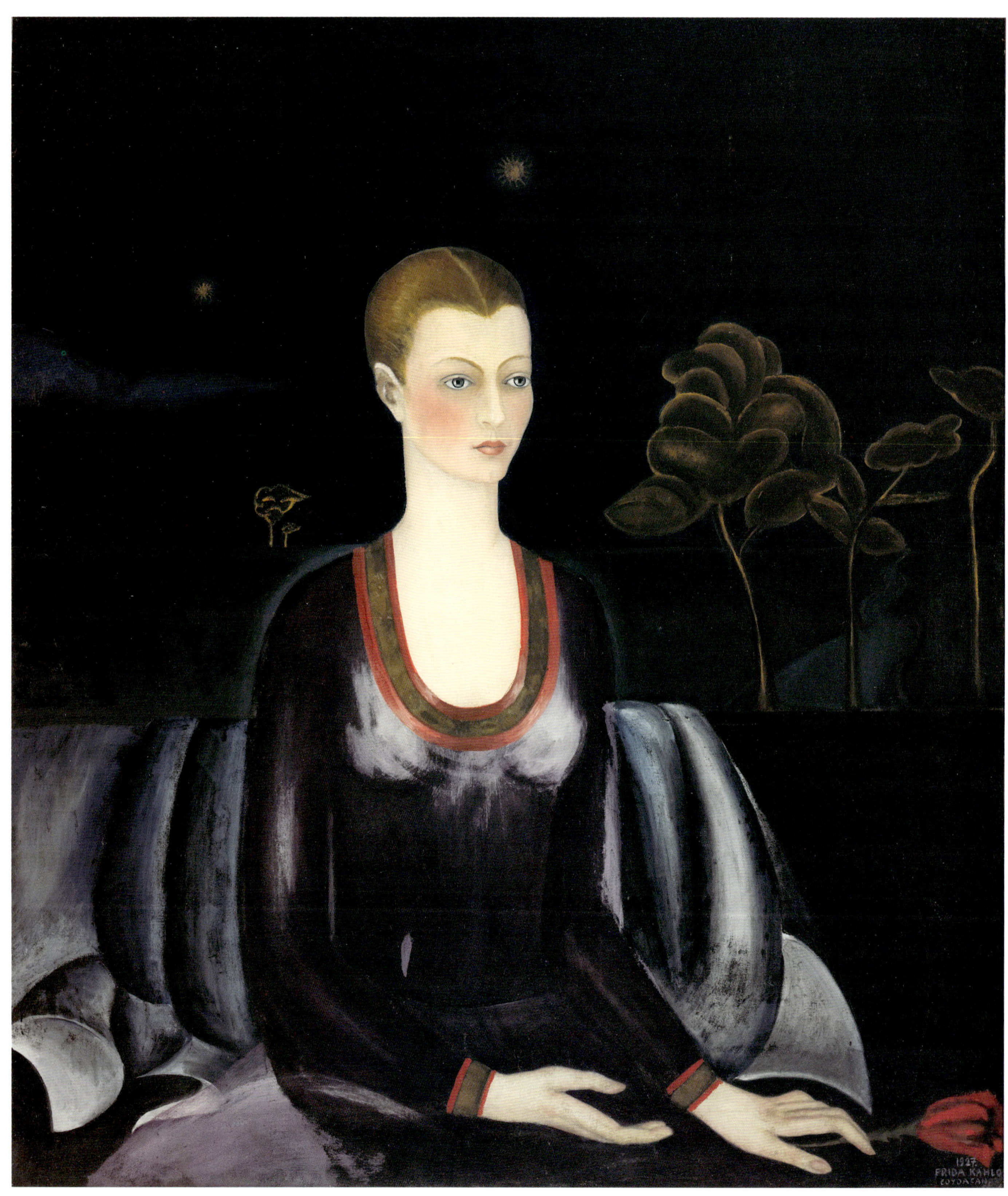

▲ Frida Kahlo *Portrait of Alicia Galant*, 1927

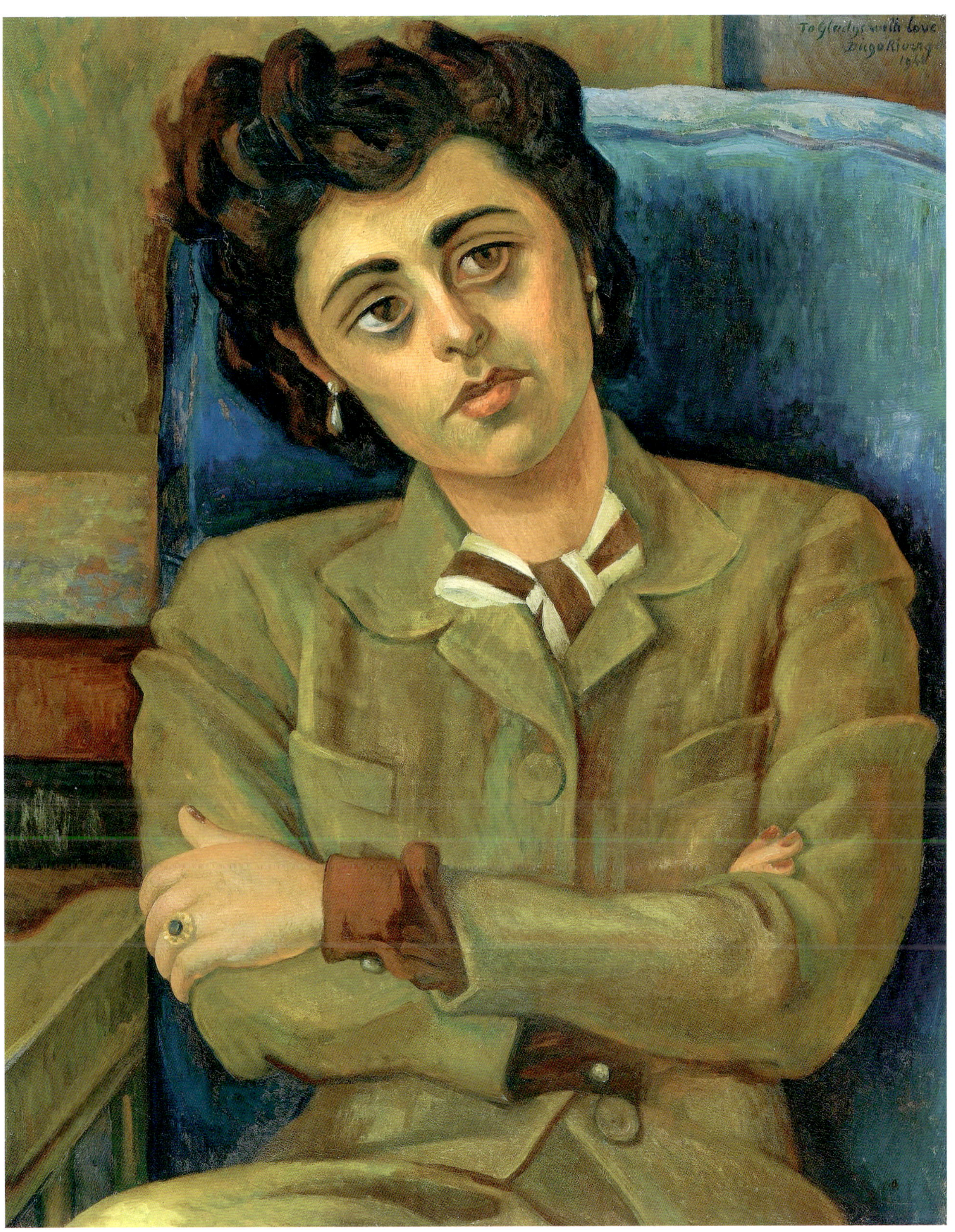

▲ Diego Rivera *Portrait of Gladys March*, 1946

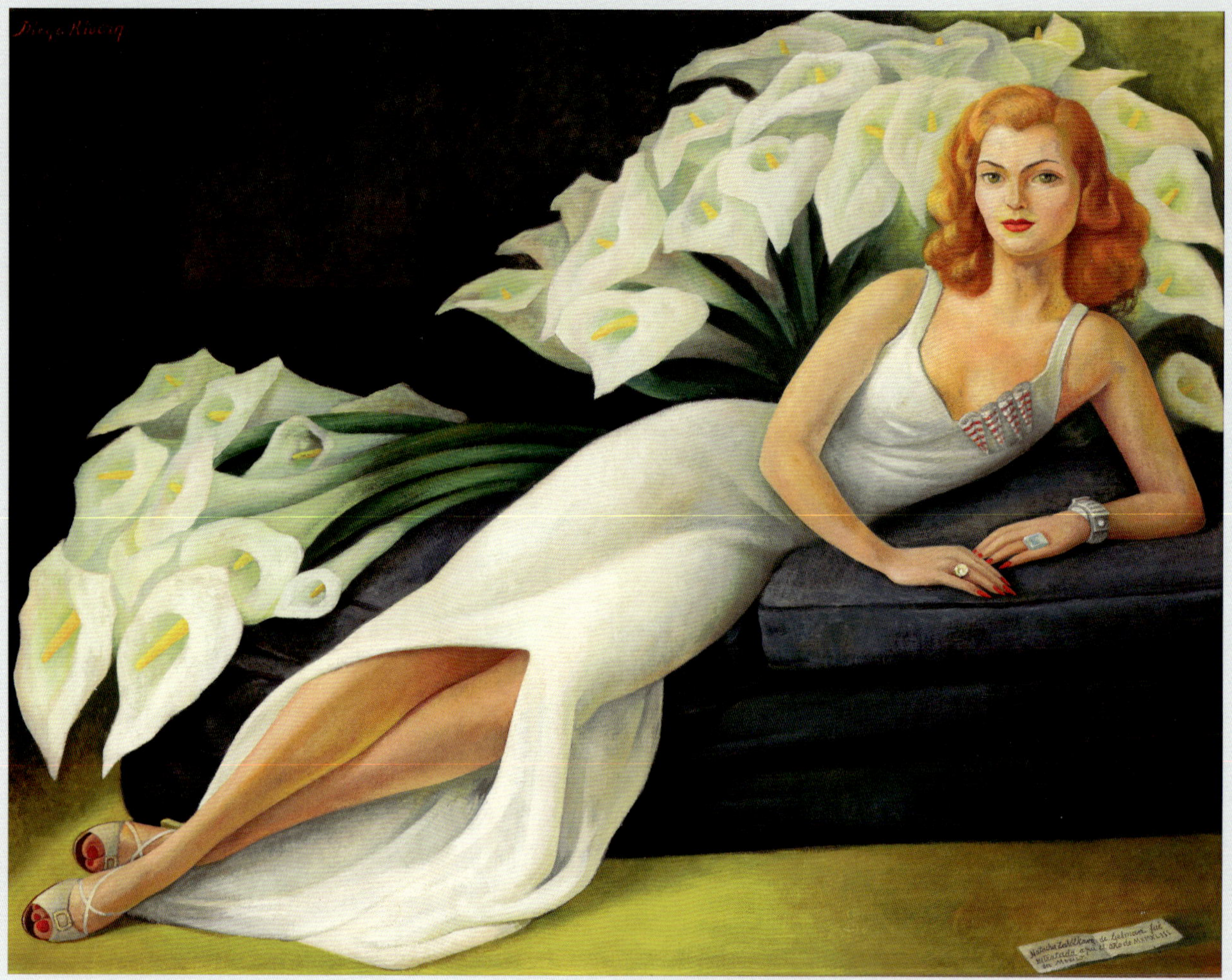

Patronage

Natasha and Jacques Gelman were great collectors of Mexican art and important patrons for Kahlo and Rivera. Born in St. Petersburg, Russia, Jacques Gelman immigrated to Mexico just before the outbreak of World War II and became a successful producer of films featuring the comedian Mario Moreno Reyes, also known as Cantinflas. Natasha Gelman (born Natasha Zahalkaha) was from Moravia in the present-day Czech Republic. While traveling the world, she found herself in Mexico City, where she met Gelman in 1939; the couple married in 1941 and quickly began amassing an extensive collection of Mexican contemporary art. Among Natasha's most prized pieces was a portrait of herself that Diego Rivera made. The painting of the young Natasha lying elegantly amidst bouquets of lilies – her white dress mirroring the shape of the flowers – hung in the salon of the Gelmans' home in Cuernavaca, Mexico.

▲ Diego Rivera *Portrait of Natasha Gelman*, 1943

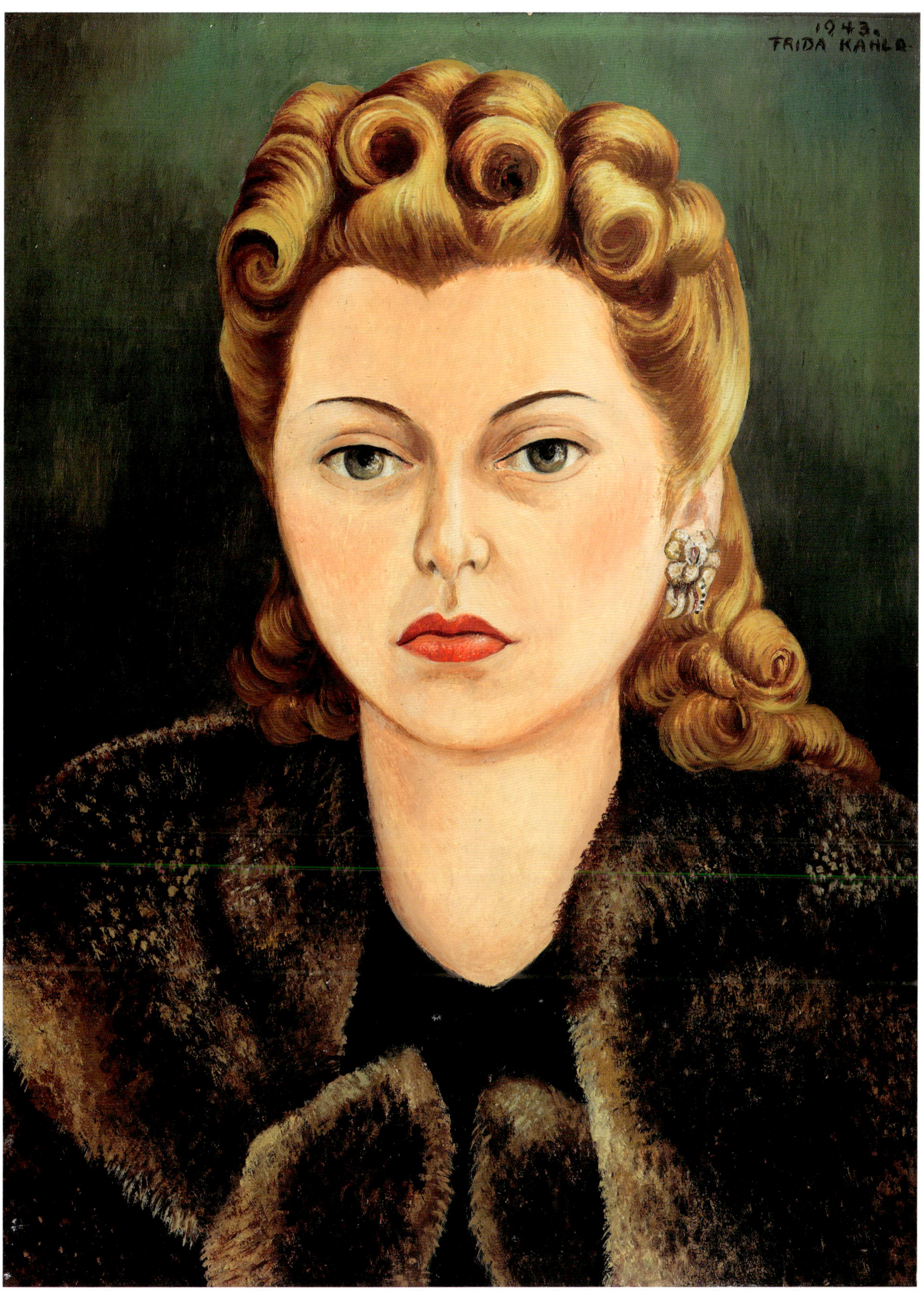

▲ Frida Kahlo *Portrait of Natasha Gelman*, 1943

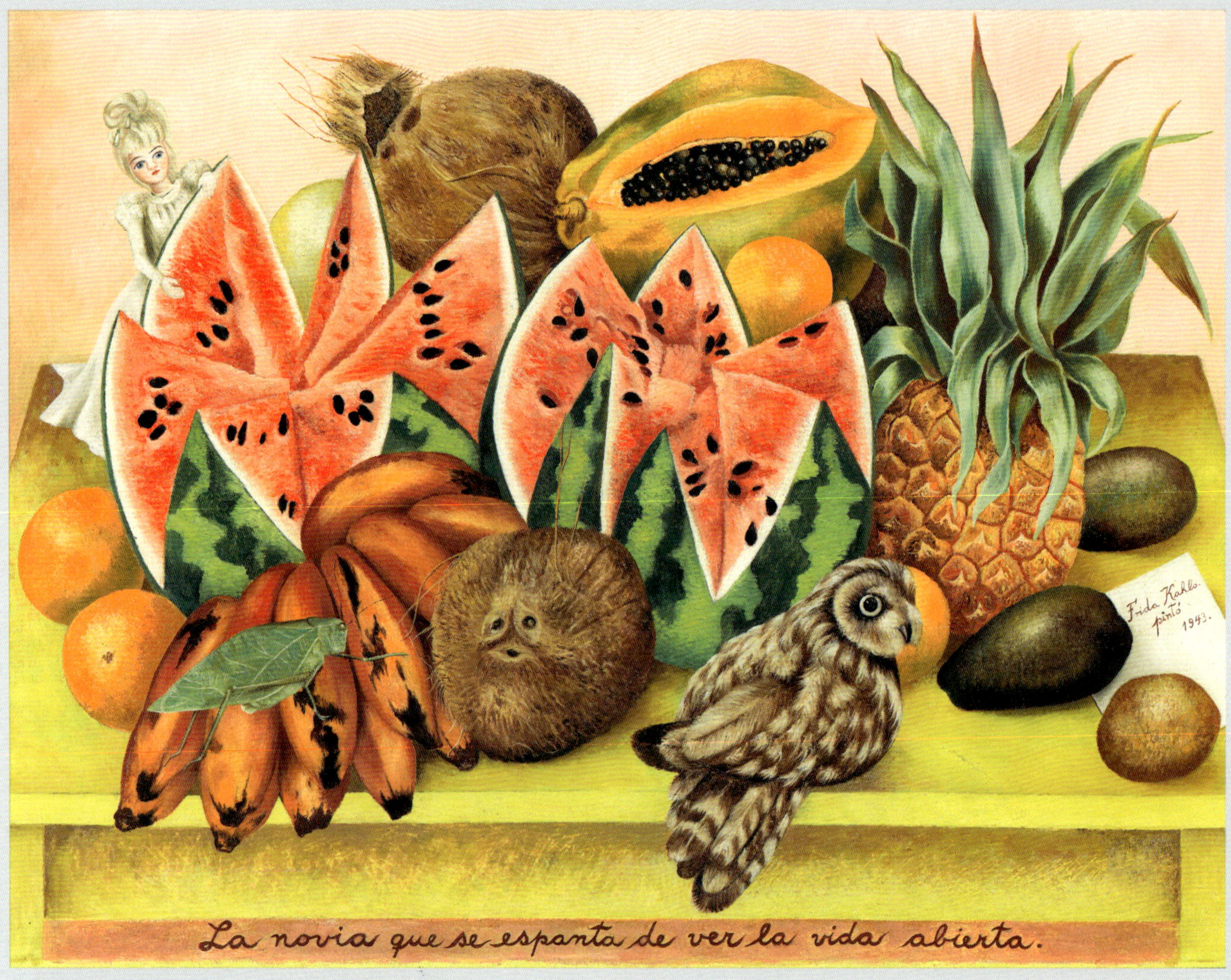

Still Lifes

Frida Kahlo's still life paintings are less well known than her self-portraits, though the approximately thirty still lifes she executed make up a relatively large percentage of her oeuvre. As with all of Kahlo's work, there is more to these fruits and freshly cut flowers than appears on the surface. In *The Bride Frightened at Seeing Life Opened* (1943), Kahlo paints a toy doll she purchased at a Paris flea market peeping nervously from an abundance of sexually charged fruit: phallic bananas, ripe papayas, and hairy coconuts. Kahlo anthropomorphized her still life subjects – coconuts shed tears and watermelons are beautifully but violently cut open to reveal their bright pink interiors. As Kahlo's health deteriorated in the late 1940s, she turned increasingly to still life painting, partly due to the practicality of being able to paint visible subjects while bedridden, but also in the spirit of *vanitas* paintings, wherein flowers and fruit represent the transience of life. She explained to Josep Bartolí in 1946, "I paint flowers so they will not die."

▲ Frida Kahlo *The Bride Frightened at Seeing Life Opened*, 1943

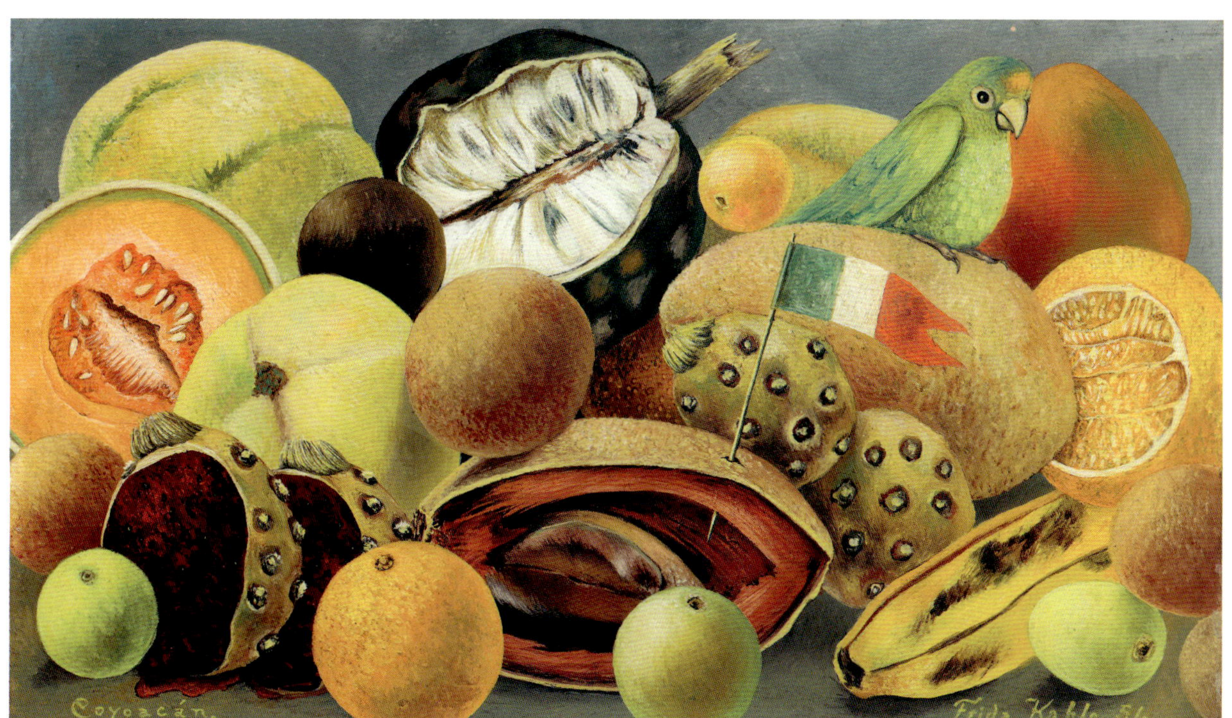

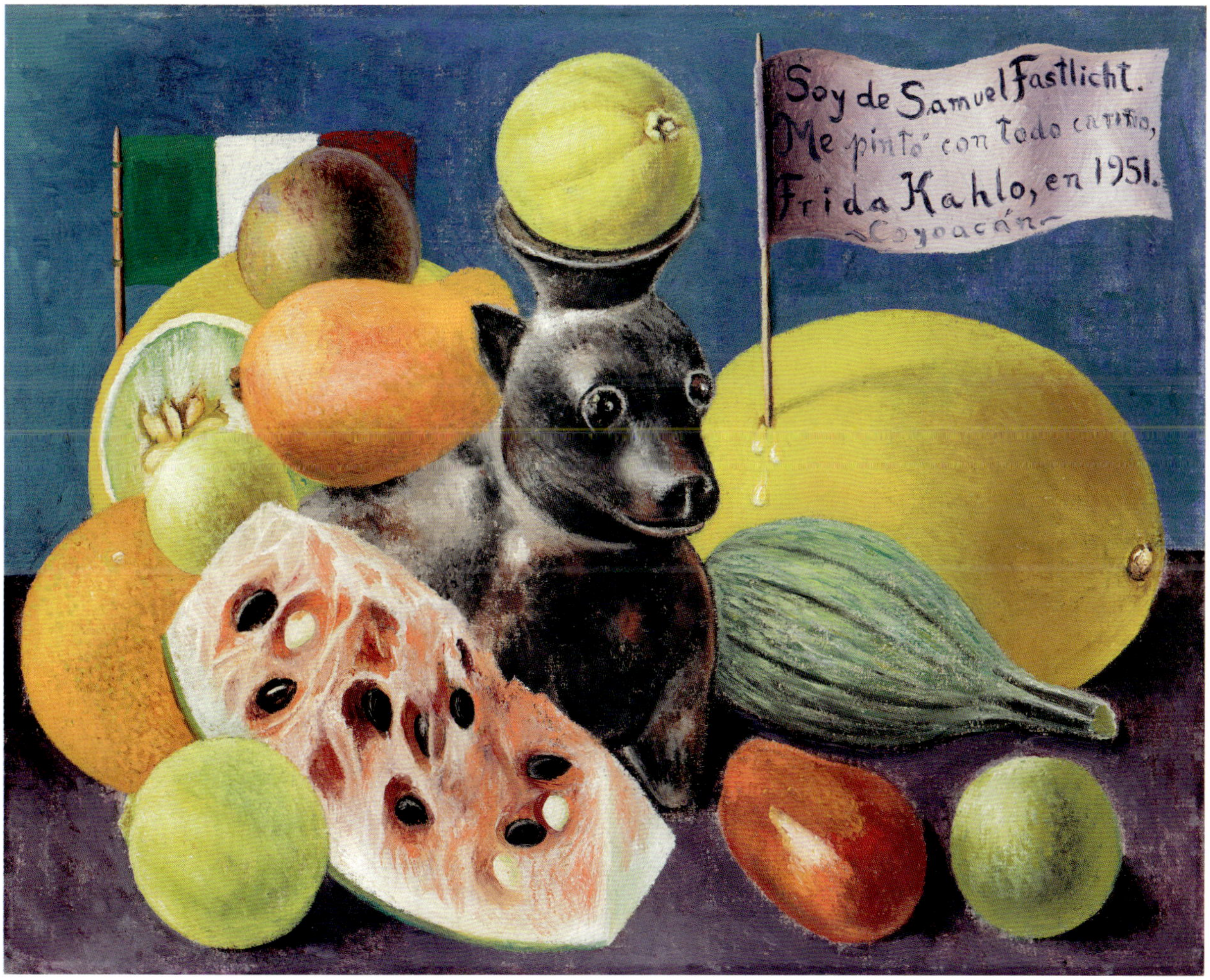

▲ Frida Kahlo *Still Life*, 1951

▲▲ Frida Kahlo *Still Life with Parrot and Flag*, 1951

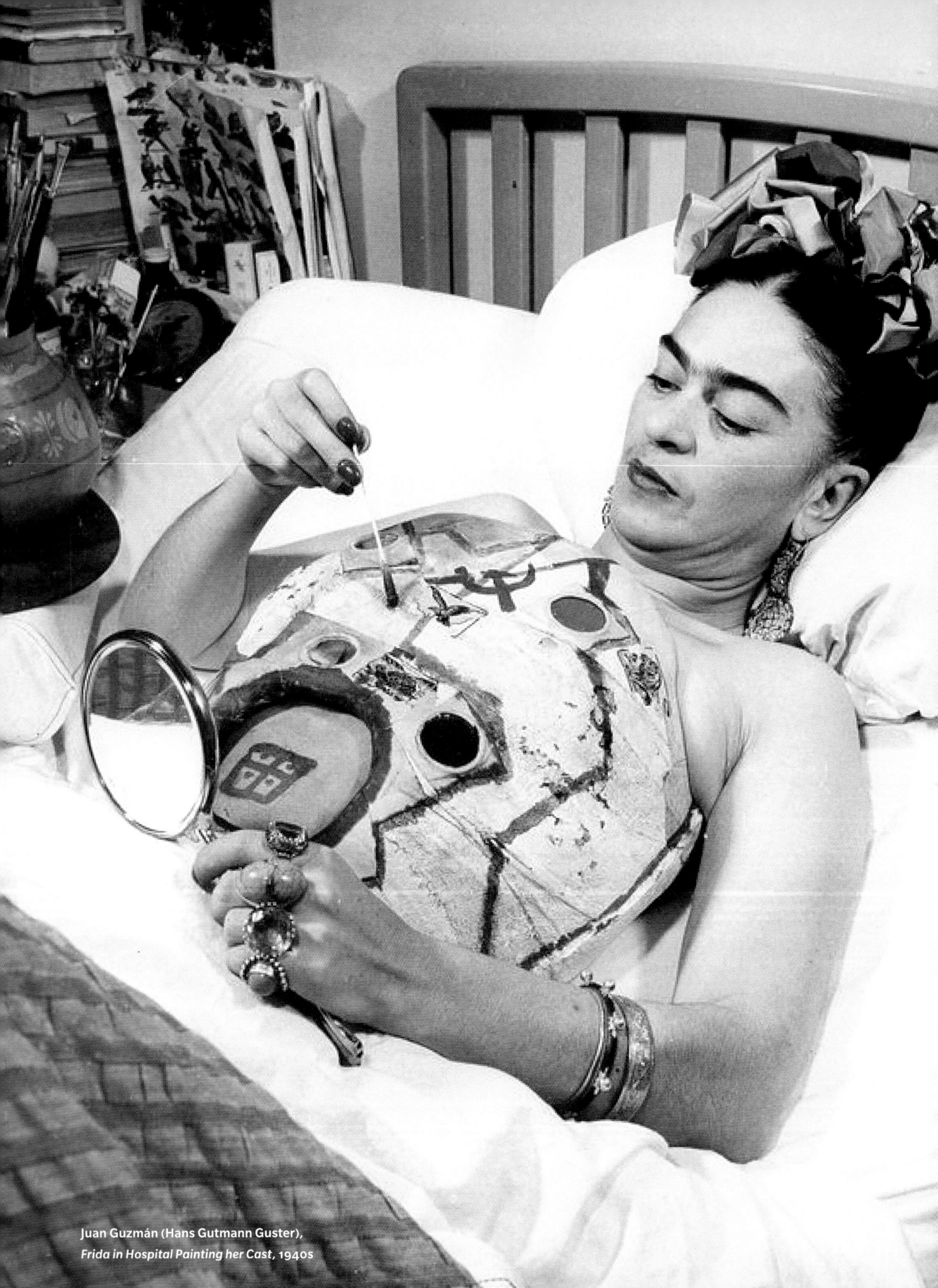

Juan Guzmán (Hans Gutmann Guster),
***Frida in Hospital Painting her Cast*, 1940s**

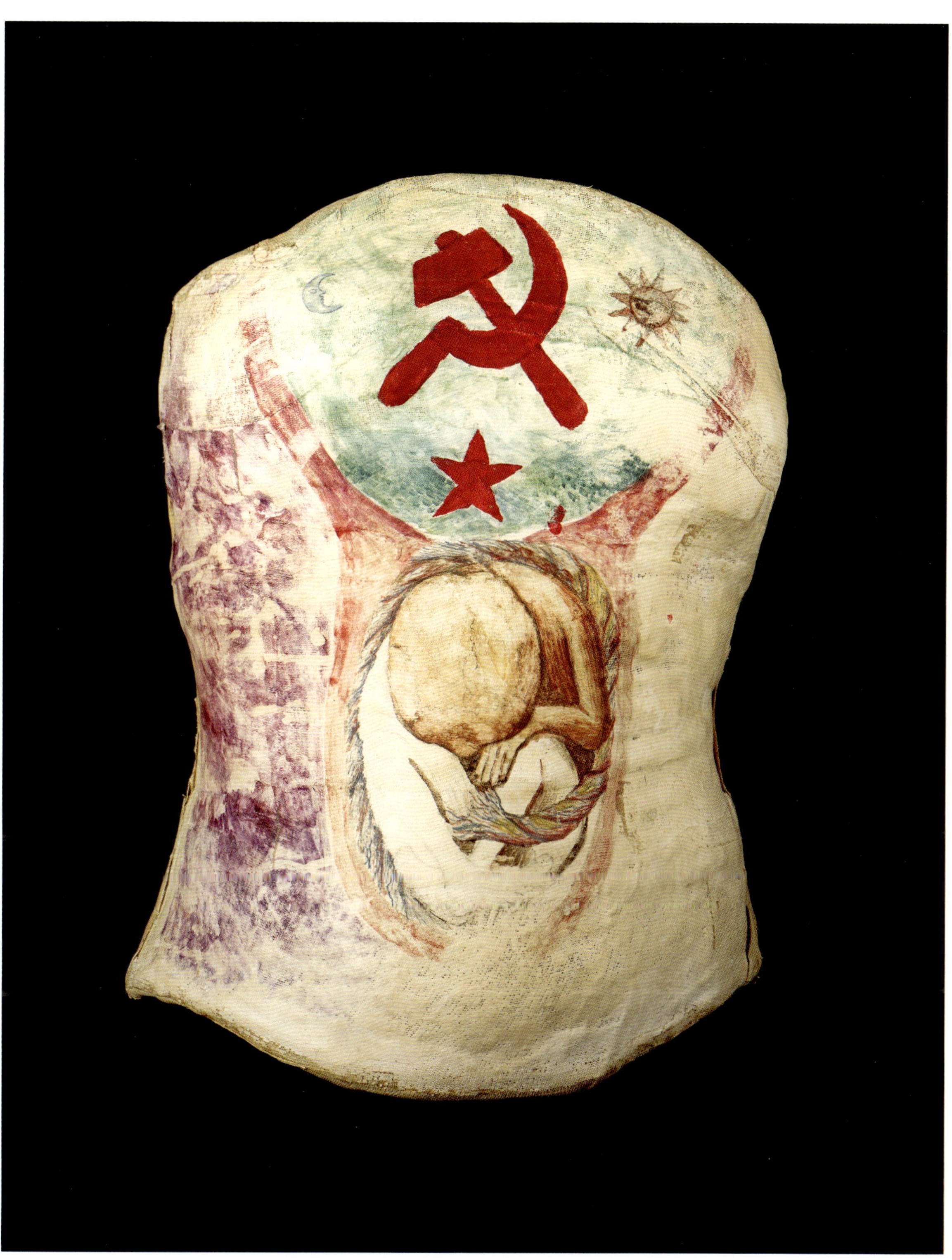

▲ Frida Kahlo *Plaster Corset with a Hammer and Sickle (An Unborn Baby)*, c. 1950

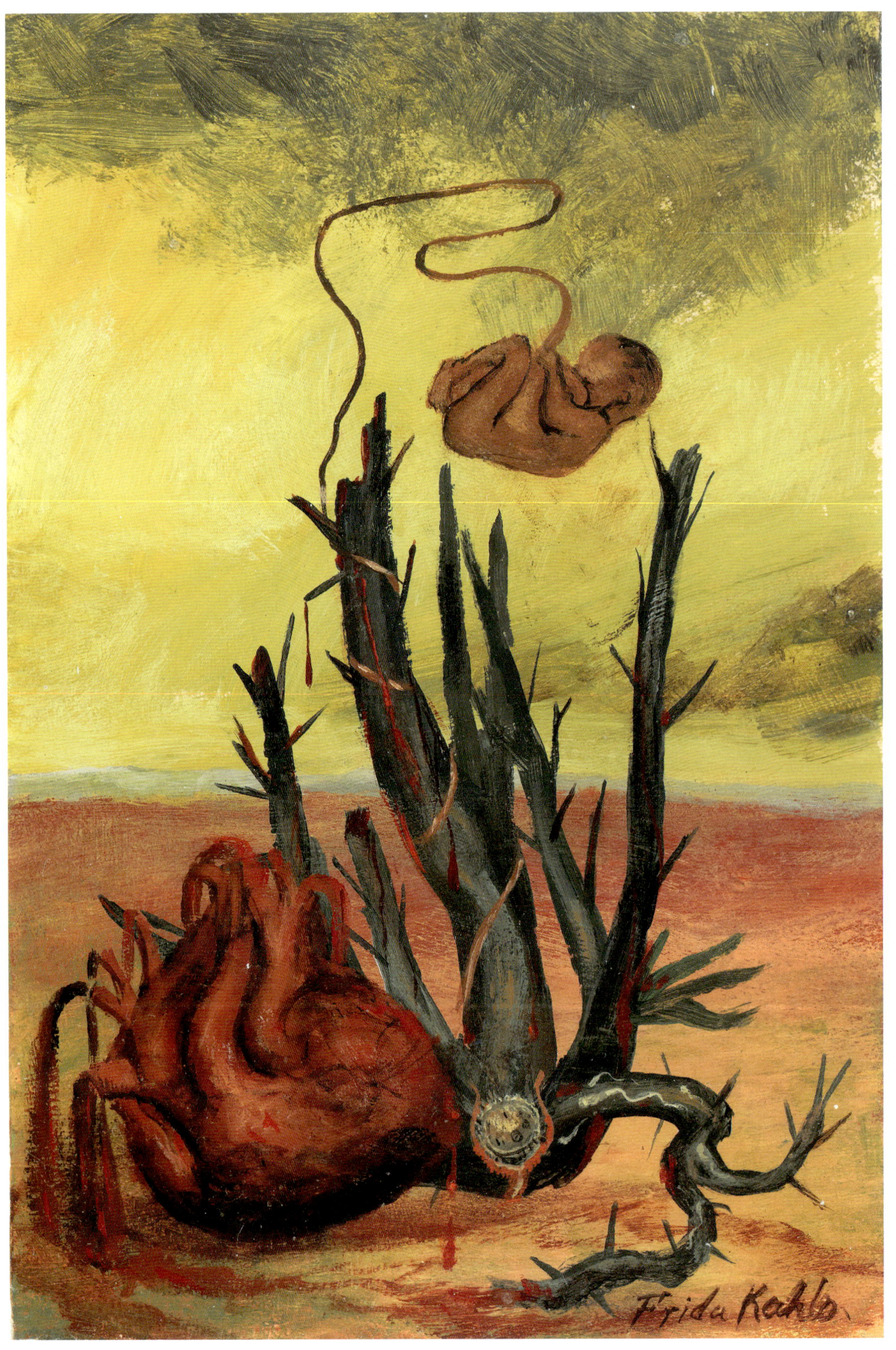

▲ Frida Kahlo *Untitled (Heart, Cactus, and Fetus)*

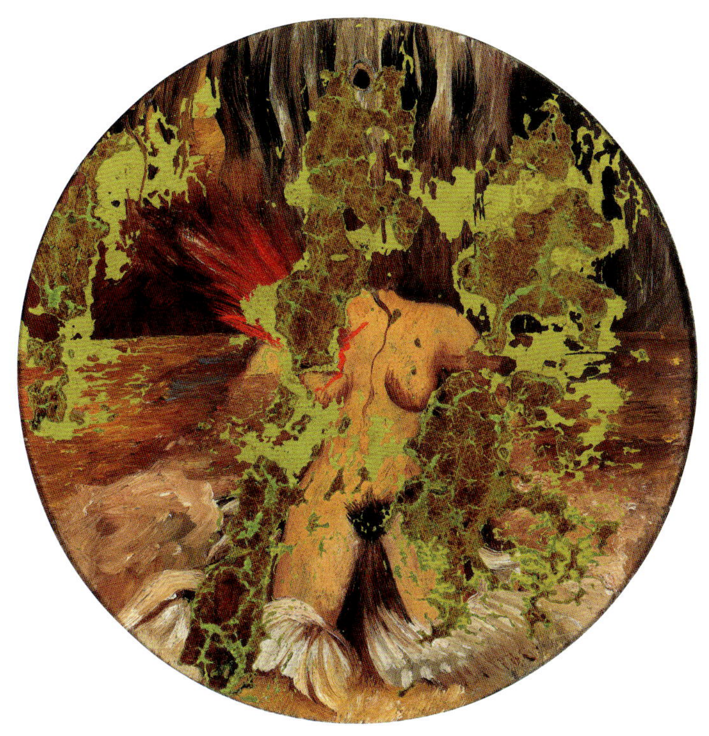

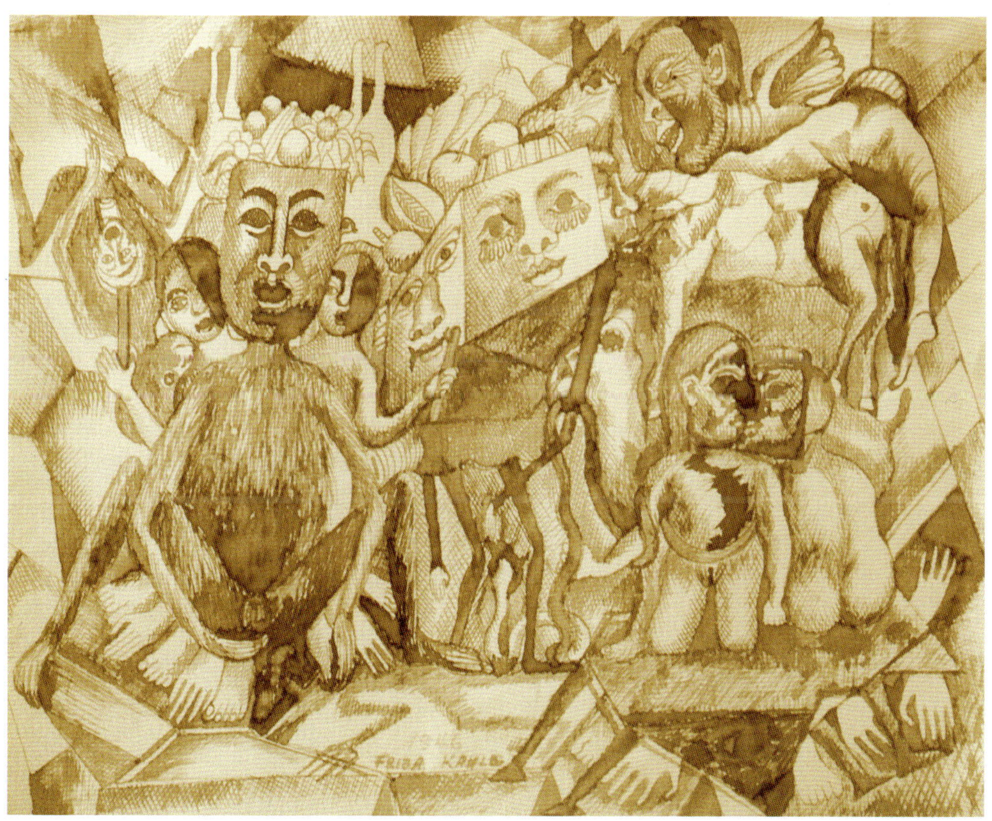

▲ Frida Kahlo *Masks*, 1946

▲▲ Frida Kahlo *The Circle*, c. 1950–1954

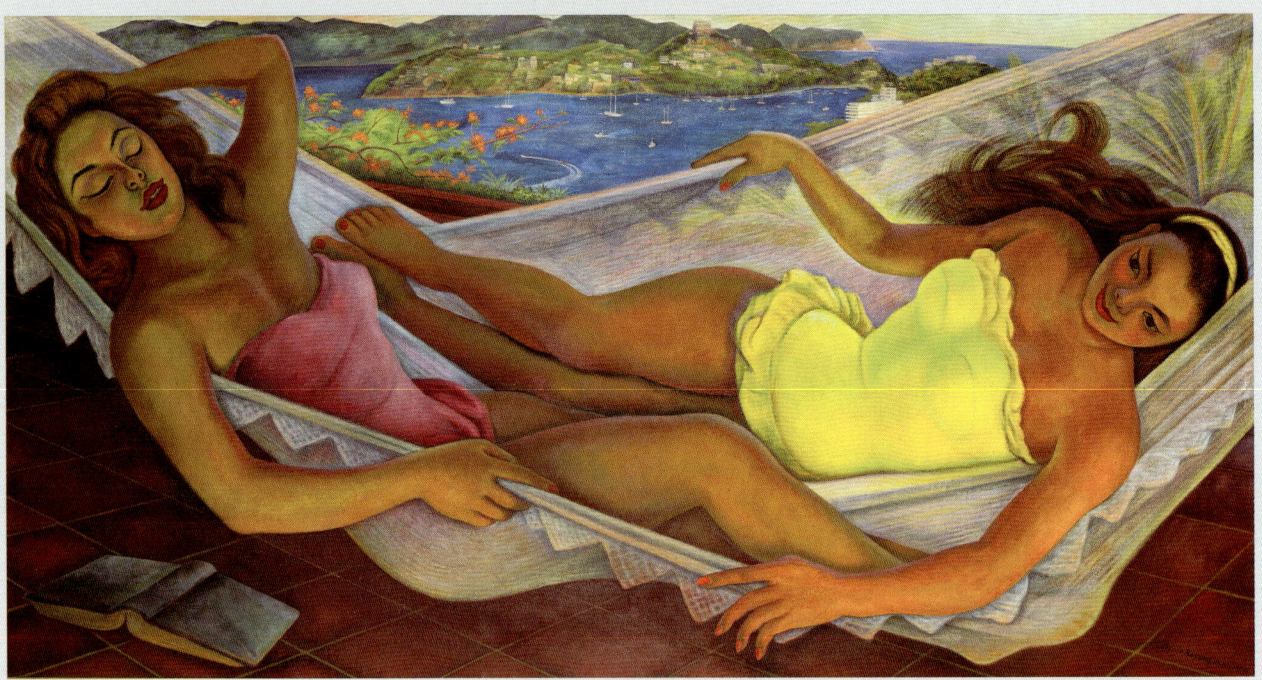

The Sunset Years

Rivera was devastated by Kahlo's death on July 13, 1954, which he later described as "the most tragic day of my life. . . . Too late now I realized that the most wonderful part of my life had been my love for Frida." Shortly after her death, he was readmitted to the Communist Party and dedicated the Casa Azul, Kahlo's family home in Coyoacán, to the Mexican people. In June 1955, Rivera was diagnosed with a recurrence of cancer. The following month he married his long-time art dealer, Emma Hurtado, and together they traveled to Moscow, where Rivera would undergo radiotherapeutic cancer treatment. After seven months he was released from the hospital, and in March 1956 he visited Poland and East Germany. Upon his return to Mexico, he painted a number of ocean sunsets – an apt metaphor signaling the end of his life – while staying at an Acapulco beach house owned by Dolores Olmedo, one of his most important patrons. He died of heart failure on November 24, 1957, at age seventy.

▲ Diego Rivera *The Hammock*, 1956

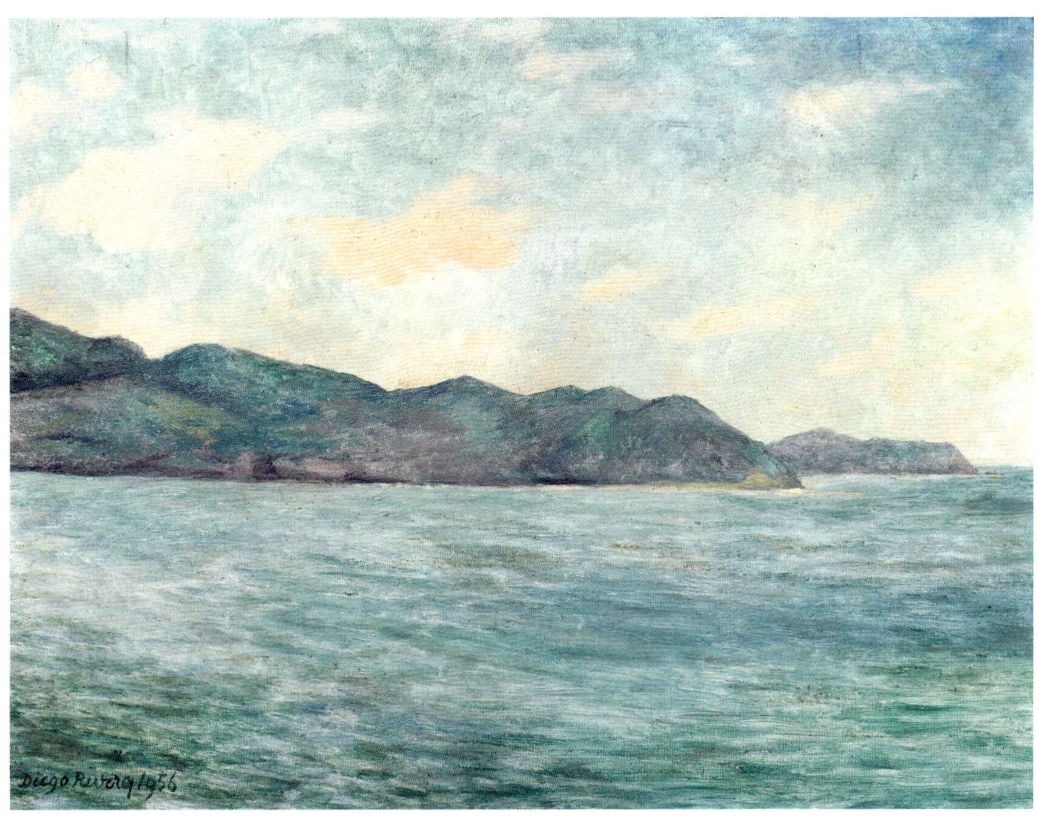

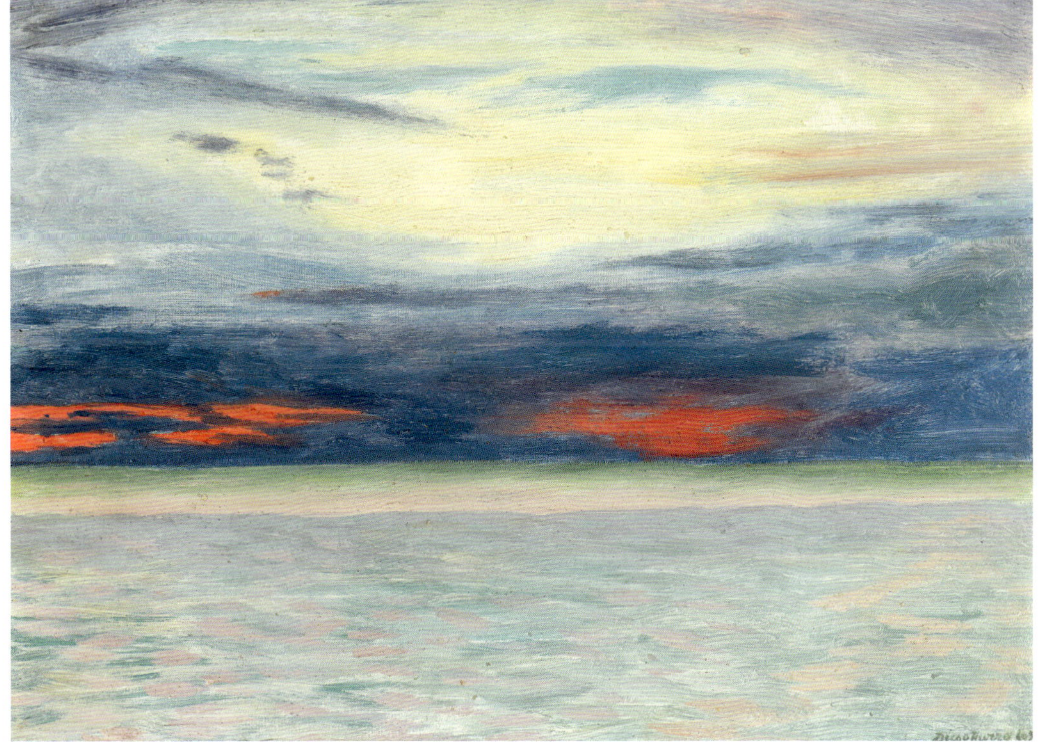

▲ Diego Rivera *Sunset 2*, 1956

▲▲ Diego Rivera *Sunset 20*, 1956

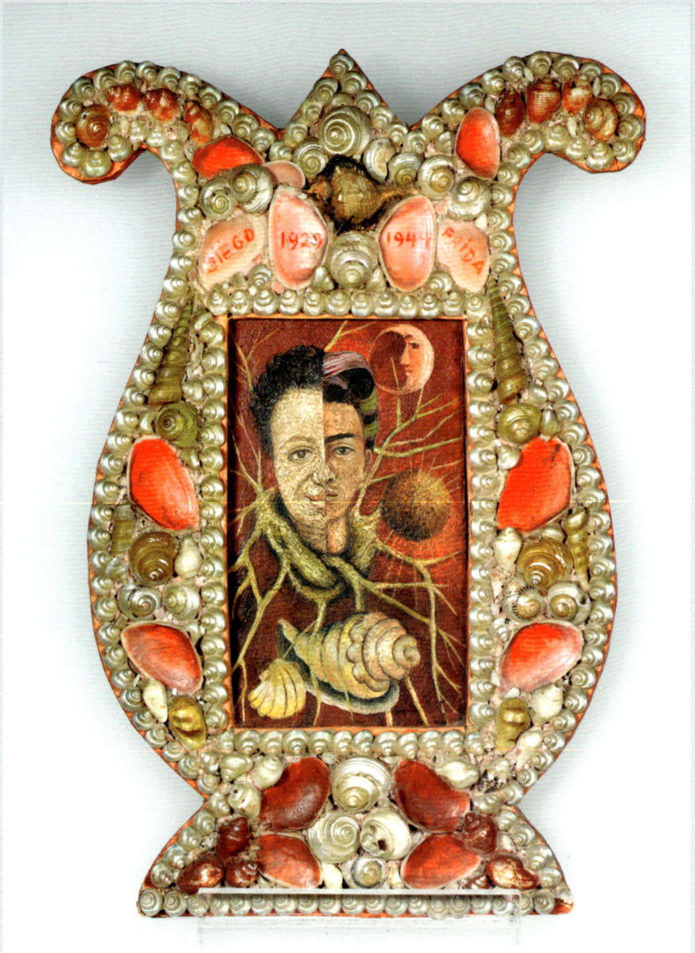

Embrace of the Universe

The Love Embrace of the Universe, the Earth (Mexico), Diego, Me, and Señor Xólotl is a rich and complex painting depicting the dichotomies of life and death, man and woman, and day and night. Kahlo presents herself in the painting's centre in the role of a Madonna, cradling Rivera like an enormous Christ Child. Rivera bears a third eye on his forehead, signifying wisdom or possibly clairvoyance. Cihuacoatl, a motherhood and fertility goddess in Aztec mythology, embraces the couple to underscore the importance Kahlo placed on Mexico for nurturing her life, creativity, and spirit. Cihuacoatl is in turn held by the Universal Mother, formed by the moon and night sky on the left, and the sun and daylight on the right. In the foreground, Kahlo's pet *Xoloitzcuintli* dog, Señor Xólotl, lies sleeping against the wrist of the Universal Mother. Here he is both her faithful companion and a symbol of the passage to the afterlife. For Kahlo, the embrace of the universe equalled her love for Rivera, as seen in *Diego and Frida 1929–1944* — an amulet-sized painting that Kahlo gave to Rivera as an anniversary present in which the two artists become one. Shortly before she died in 1954, she declared to a journalist that Diego "is my child, my son, my mother, my father, my husband, my everything."

▲ Frida Kahlo *Diego and Frida, 1929–1944*, 1944

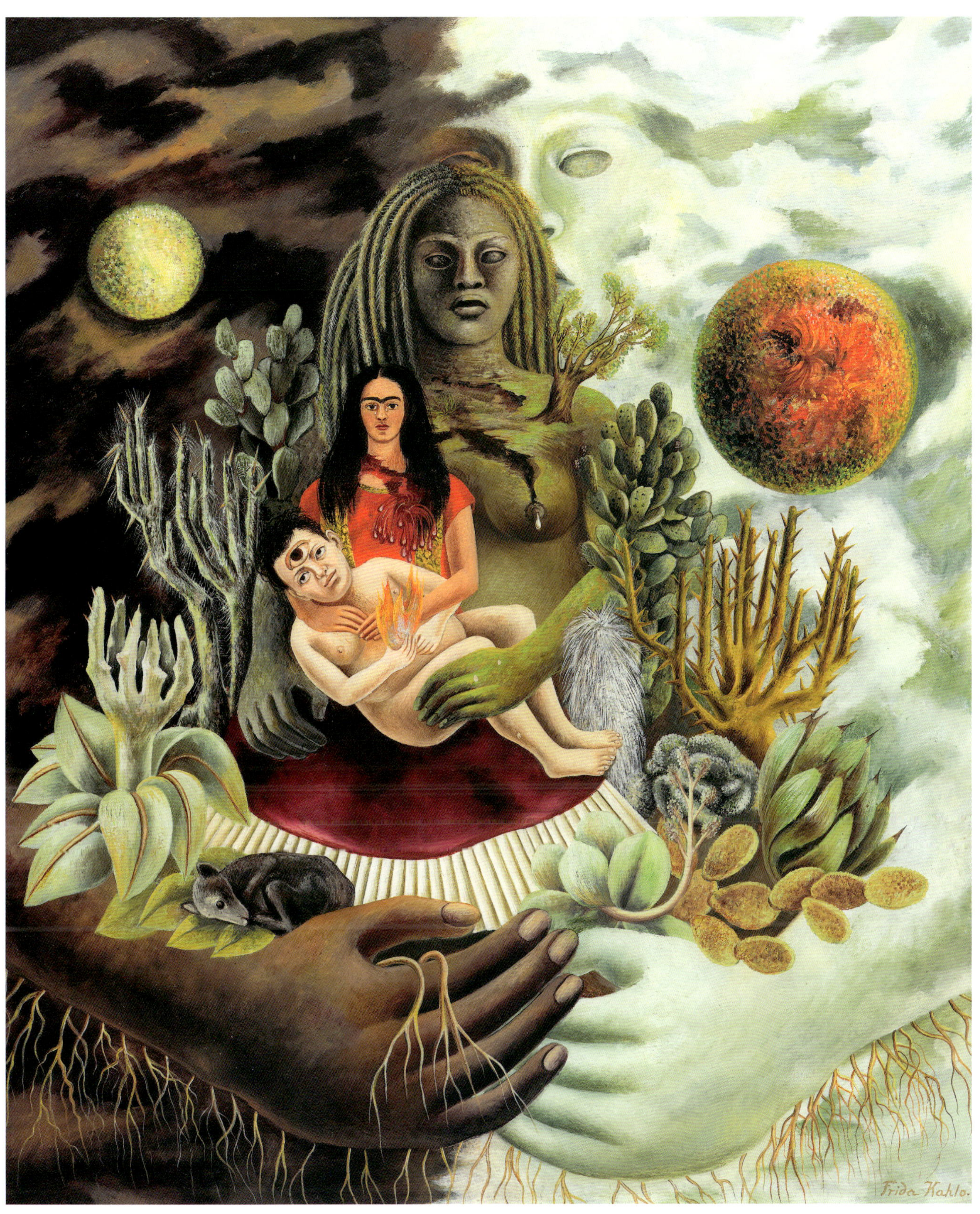

Frida Kahlo *The Love Embrace of the Universe, the Earth (Mexico), Diego, Me, and Señor Xólotl*, 1949

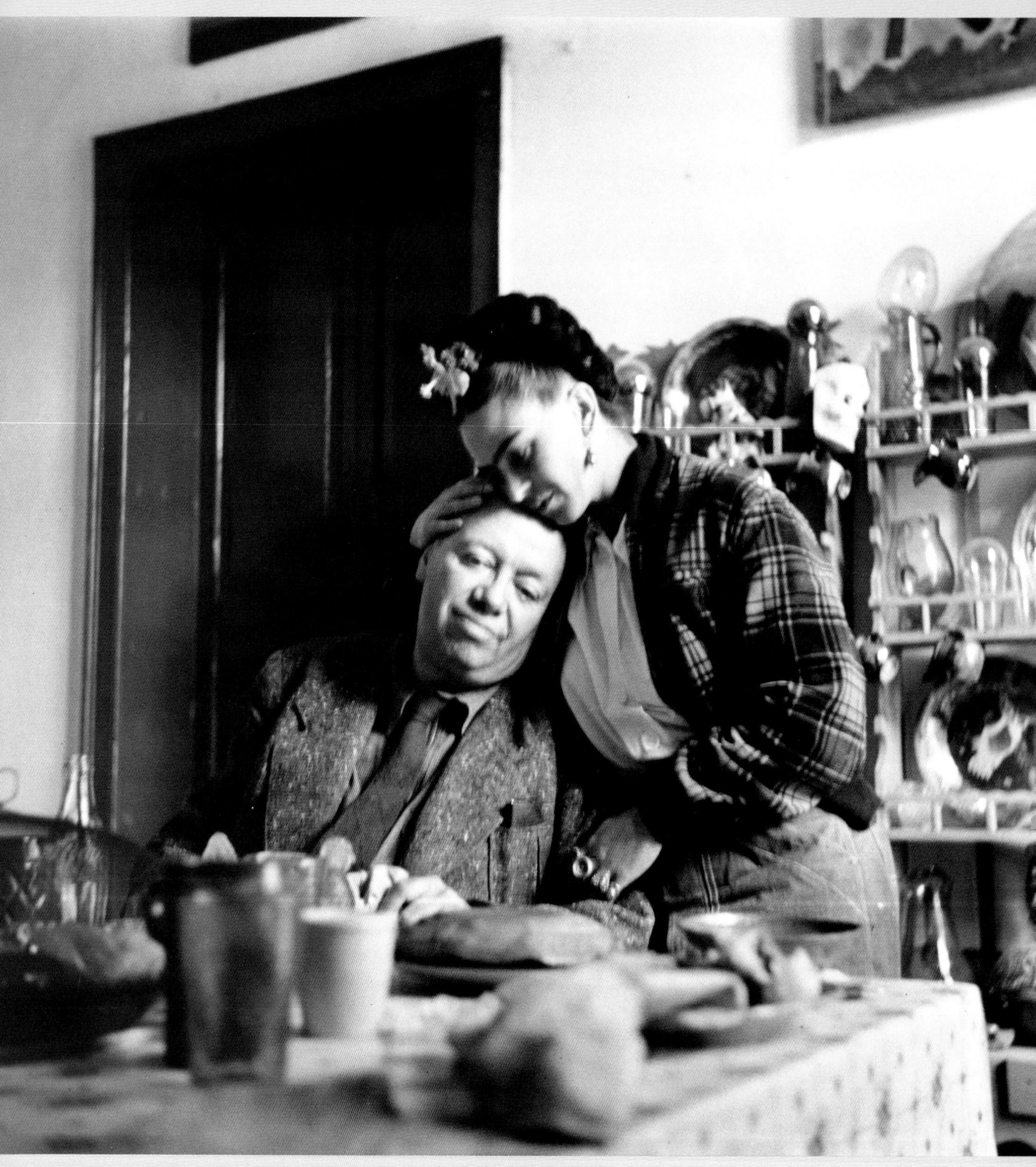

Emmy Lou Packard, *Frida Kahlo and Diego Rivera*, 1941

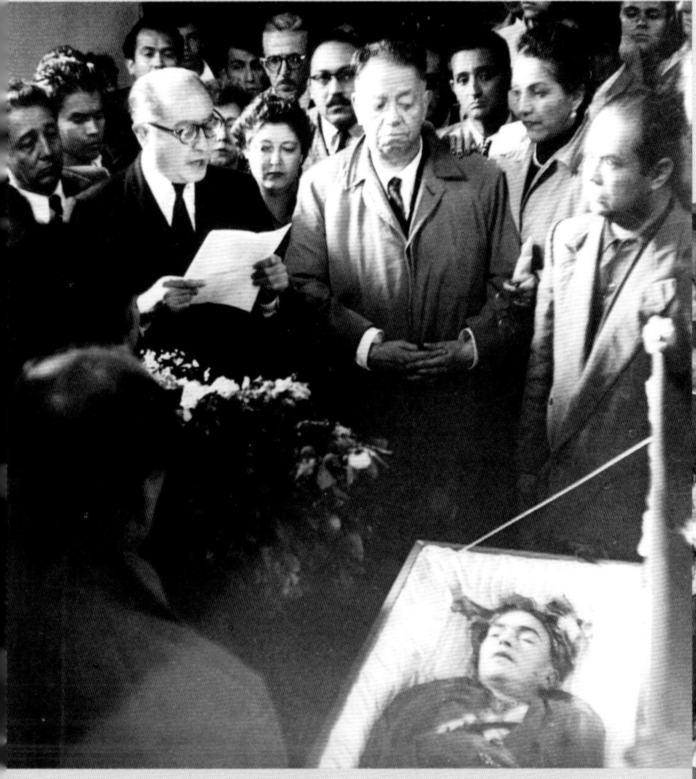

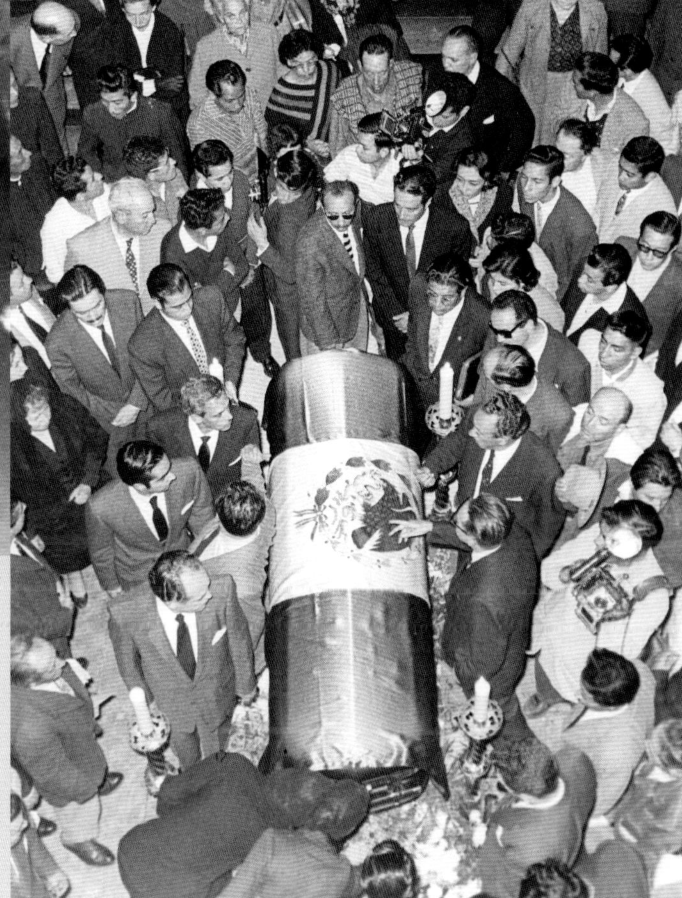

Héctor García, *Frida Kahlo in Coffin with Diego Rivera at Funeral*, 1954

G.Y. Massart, *Diego Rivera's Funeral*, 1957

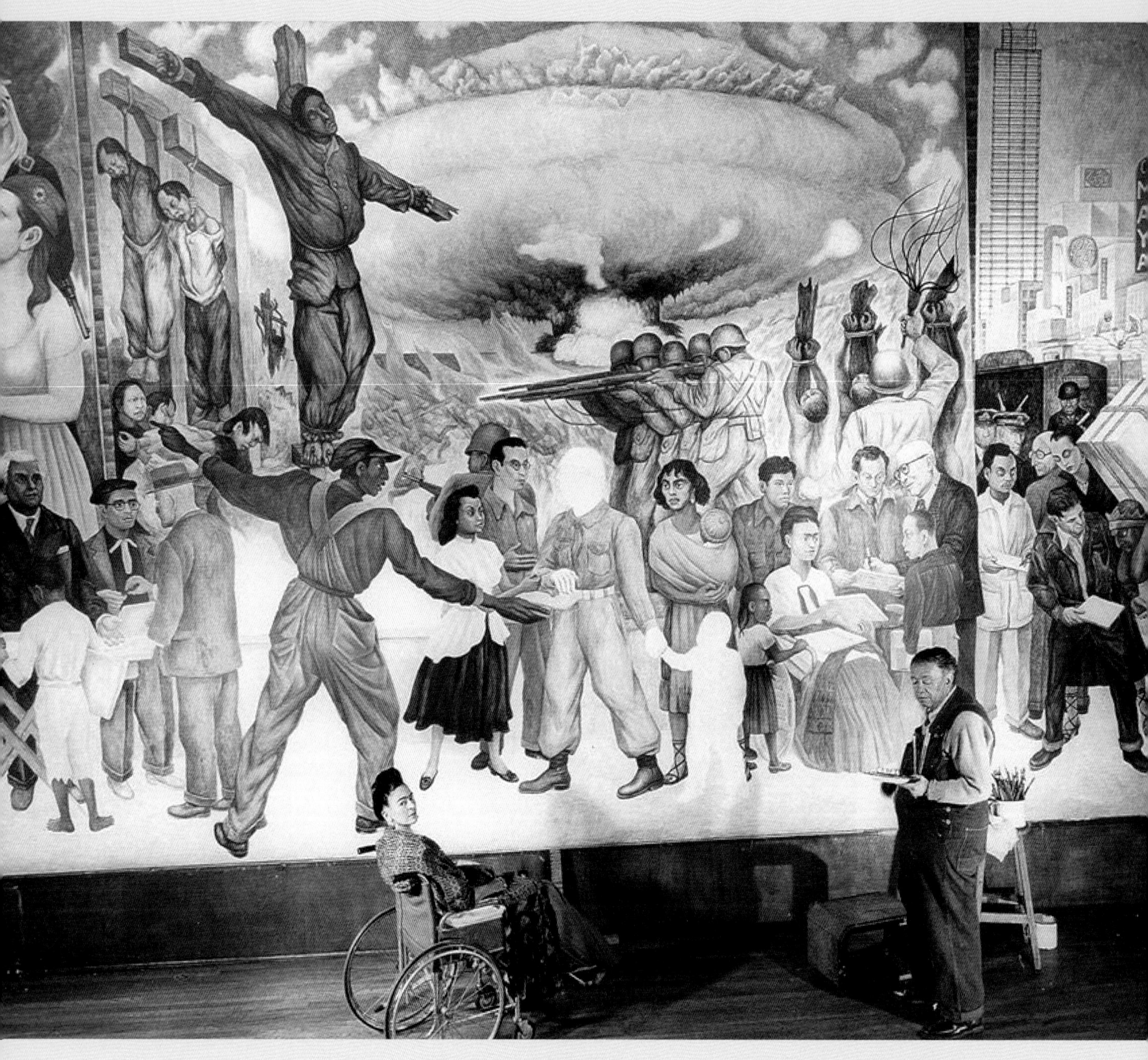

Juan Guzmán (Hans Gutmann Guster),
Untitled – Frida Posing for Diego Rivera's Mural
The Nightmare of War and the Dream of Peace *in the Palacio de Bellas Artes, Mexico*, 1952

LIST OF WORKS
IN CHRONOLOGICAL ORDER

Frida Kahlo
born and died Mexico City, Mexico, 1907–1954

Retrato de Alicia Galant
Portrait of Alicia Galant
1927
oil on canvas
43 x 37 inches (108.0 x 93.5 cm)
Collection of Museo Dolores Olmedo, Xochimilco, México
Page 70

El camión
The Bus
1929
oil on canvas
10 x 22 inches (26.0 x 55.5 cm)
Collection of Museo Dolores Olmedo, Xochimilco, México
Page 44

Desnudo de Eva Frederick
Nude of Eva Frederick
1931
pencil and charcoal on paper
24 x 19 inches (61.5 x 48.5 cm)
Collection of Museo Dolores Olmedo, Xochimilco, México

Retrato de Lady Hastings
Portrait of Lady Hastings
1931
colored pencil on paper
19 x 12 inches (48.0 x 31.0 cm)
Collection of Museo Dolores Olmedo, Xochimilco, México

Retrato de Luther Burbank
Portrait of Luther Burbank
1931
oil on Masonite
34 x 24 inches (87.0 x 62.0 cm)
Collection of Museo Dolores Olmedo, Xochimilco, México
Page 68

Frida y el aborto
Frida and the Abortion
1932
lithograph on paper
12½ x 9½ inches (31.7 x 24.0 cm)
Collection of Museo Dolores Olmedo, Xochimilco, México

Hospital Henry Ford
Henry Ford Hospital
1932
oil on metal
12 x 15 inches (31.0 x 38.5 cm)
Collection of Museo Dolores Olmedo, Xochimilco, México
Page 47

*Mi vestido cuelga aqui**
My Dress Hangs Here
1933
oil and collage on Masonite
18 x 20 inches (45.5 x 50.5 cm)
Collection of FEMSA
Page 42

Autorretrato con collar
Self-Portrait with Necklace
1933
oil on metal
14 x 11 inches (35.0 x 29.0 cm)
The Jacques and Natasha Gelman Collection of Mexican Art
Page 7

Unos cuantos piquetitos
A Few Small Nips
1935
oil on metal
15 x 19 inches (38.0 x 48.5 cm)
Collection of Museo Dolores Olmedo, Xochimilco, México
Page 46

Mi Nana y yo
My Nurse and I
1937
oil on metal
12 x 14 inches (30.5 x 35.0 cm)
Collection of Museo Dolores Olmedo, Xochimilco, México
Page 50

Retrato de Diego Rivera
Portrait of Diego Rivera
1937
oil on Masonite
21 x 15 inches (53.0 x 39.0 cm)
The Jacques and Natasha Gelman Collection of Mexican Art
Page 6

Autorretrato sentada en la cama (Yo y mi muñeca)
Self-Portrait Sitting on the Bed (Me and My Doll)
1937
oil on metal
16 x 12 inches (40.0 x 30.0 cm)
The Jacques and Natasha Gelman Collection of Mexican Art
Page 57

El difuntito Dimas Rosas, a los tres años de edad
The Deceased Dimas Rosas, Aged Three
1937
oil on Masonite
19 x 12 inches (48.0 x 31.5 cm)
Collection of Museo Dolores Olmedo, Xochimilco, México
Page 58

Autorretrato con mono
Self-Portrait with Monkey
1938
oil on Masonite
16 x 12 inches (40.5 x 30.5 cm)
Collection Albright-Knox Art Gallery, Buffalo, New York. Bequest of A. Conger Goodyear, 1966. Photo: Albright-Knox Art Gallery/Art Resource, NY
Page 54

*Works exhibited at the High Museum of Art only

Autorretrato con pelo cortado
Self-Portrait with Cropped Hair
1940
oil on canvas
16 x 11 inches (40.0 x 28.0 cm)
The Museum of Modern Art, New York. Gift of Edgar Kaufmann, Jr., 1943. Digital Image © The Museum of Modern Art/Licensed by SCALA/Art Resource, NY
Page 56

Autorretrato con trenza
Self-Portrait with Braid
1941
oil on canvas
20 x 15 inches (51.0 x 38.5 cm)
The Jacques and Natasha Gelman Collection of Mexican Art
Page 55

Autorretrato con vestido rojo y dorado
Self-Portrait with Red and Gold Dress
1941
oil on canvas
15 x 11 inches (39.0 x 27.5 cm)
The Jacques and Natasha Gelman Collection of Mexican Art
Page 51

Retrato de Natasha Gelman
Portrait of Natasha Gelman
1943
oil on Masonite
12 x 9 inches (30.0 x 23.0 cm)
The Jacques and Natasha Gelman Collection of Mexican Art
Page 73

Autorretrato como Tehuana (Diego en mi pensamiento)
Self-Portrait as a Tehuana (Diego in My Thoughts)
1943
oil on Masonite
30 x 24 inches (76.0 x 61.0 cm)
The Jacques and Natasha Gelman Collection of Mexican Art
Page 49

Autorretrato con monos
Self-Portrait with Monkeys
1943
oil on canvas
32 x 25 inches (81.5 x 63.0 cm)
The Jacques and Natasha Gelman Collection of Mexican Art
Page 52

La novia que se espanta de ver la vida abierta
The Bride Frightened at Seeing Life Opened
1943
oil on canvas
25 x 32 inches (63.0 x 81.5 cm)
The Jacques and Natasha Gelman Collection of Mexican Art
Page 74

Diego y Frida, 1929–1944
Diego and Frida, 1929–1944
1944
oil on wood
10 x 7 inches (26.0 x 18.5 cm)
Private collection, courtesy of Galería Arvil, México
Page 82

Retrato de Doña Rosita Morillo
Portrait of Doña Rosita Morillo
1944
oil on canvas
30 x 24 inches (76.0 x 61.0 cm)
Collection of Museo Dolores Olmedo, Xochimilco, México
Page 69

La columna rota
The Broken Column
1944
oil on canvas
16 x 12 inches (40.0 x 30.5 cm)
Collection of Museo Dolores Olmedo, Xochimilco, México
Page 45

La flor de la vida
The Flower of Life
1944
oil on Masonite
11 x 8 inches (28.0 x 20.0 cm)
Collection of Museo Dolores Olmedo, Xochimilco, México
Page 66

Autorretrato con changuito
Self-Portrait with Monkey
1945
oil on Masonite
22 x 16 inches (56.0 x 41.5 cm)
Collection of Museo Dolores Olmedo, Xochimilco, México
Page 53

Sin esperanza
Without Hope
1945
oil on canvas
11 x 14 inches (28.0 x 36.0 cm)
Collection of Museo Dolores Olmedo, Xochimilco, México
Page 65

11:25
1946
sepia ink on paper
11 x 7½ inches (28.0 x 19.0 cm)
The Jacques and Natasha Gelman Collection of Mexican Art

Dharma chakra
1946
sepia ink on paper
7 x 11 inches (18.0 x 27.0 cm)
The Jacques and Natasha Gelman Collection of Mexican Art

Máscaras
Masks
1946
sepia ink on paper
8½ x 11 inches (21.5 x 27.0 cm)
The Jacques and Natasha Gelman Collection of Mexican Art
Page 79

El abrazo de amor del universo, la Tierra (México), Diego, yo y el señor Xólotl
The Love Embrace of the Universe, the Earth (Mexico), Diego, Me, and Señor Xólotl
1949
oil on Masonite
28 x 24 inches (70.0 x 60.5 cm)
The Jacques and Natasha Gelman Collection of Mexican Art
Page 83

Plaster Corset with a Hammer and Sickle (An Unborn Baby)
c. 1950
dry plaster and mixed media
16½ x 5½ inches (42.0 x 14.0 cm)
Courtesy of Artemundi Group, Javier Lumbreras
Page 77

El círculo
The Circle
c. 1950–1954
oil on metal
6 inches in diameter (15 cm)
Collection of Museo Dolores Olmedo, Xochimilco, México
Page 79

Naturaleza muerta
Still Life
1951
oil on canvas
11 x 14 inches (28.5 x 36.0 cm)
Private collection, courtesy of Galería Arvil, México
Page 75

Naturaleza muerta con perico y bandera
Still Life with Parrot and Flag
1951
oil on Masonite
10 x 14 inches (26.0 x 35.0 cm)
Private collection, courtesy of Galería Arvil, México
Page 75

"Fantasmones siniestros", página del diario (anverso y reverso)
"Sinister Phantasms", Page from Diary (recto and verso)
watercolor, crayon, pencil, and pen and ink on paper
9 x 6 inches (23.0 x 14.5 cm)
The Jacques and Natasha Gelman Collection of Mexican Art

Sin título (corazón, cactus, y feto)
Untitled (Heart, Cactus, and Fetus)
oil on parchment
6 x 4 inches (15.5 x 10.5 cm)
Collection of Museo Dolores Olmedo, Xochimilco, México
Page 78

Diego Rivera
born Guanajuato, Mexico, 1886; died Mexico City, Mexico, 1957

Autorretrato con chambergo
Self-Portrait with Wide-Brimmed Hat
1907
oil on canvas
33 x 24 inches (84.5 x 61.5 cm)
Collection of Museo Dolores Olmedo, Xochimilco, México
Page 22

El picador
The Bullfighter
1909
oil on canvas
70 x 44½ inches (177.0 x 113.0 cm)
Collection of Museo Dolores Olmedo, Xochimilco, México
Page 28

El sol rompiendo la bruma (El viaducto de Meudon)
Sun Breaking through the Mist (The Road to Meudon)
1913
oil on canvas
33 x 23 inches (83.5 x 59.0 cm)
Collection of Museo Dolores Olmedo, Xochimilco, México
Page 26

Alquerías
Farmhouses
1914
oil on canvas
27½ x 31½ inches (70.0 x 80.0 cm)
Collection of Museo Dolores Olmedo, Xochimilco, México

*El grande de España (El ángel azul)**
The Noble of Spain (The Blue Angel)
1914
oil on canvas
76 x 51 inches (194 x 130 cm)
Collection of FEMSA

El joven de la estilográfica (Retrato de Best Maugard)
Young Man with a Fountain Pen (Portrait of Best Maugard)
1914
oil on canvas
31 x 25 inches (79.5 x 63.5 cm)
Collection of Museo Dolores Olmedo, Xochimilco, México
Page 23

No. 9, Nature morte espagnole
Spanish Still Life, No. 9
1915
oil on canvas
36 x 43½ inches (90.5 x 110.5 cm)
National Gallery of Art, Washington, DC. Gift of Katharine Graham, 2002
Page 25

El rastro
The Flea Market
1915
oil on canvas
11 x 15 inches (27.5 x 38.5 cm)
Collection of Museo Dolores Olmedo, Xochimilco, México

Última hora
The Last Hour
1915
oil on canvas
36 x 29 inches (92.0 x 73.0 cm)
The Jacques and Natasha Gelman Collection of Mexican Art

Naturaleza muerta en ovalo
Oval Still Life
c. 1915–1916
oil on canvas
36½ x 31 inches (93.0 x 79.0 cm)
Collection of Michael Audain and Yoshiko Karasawa

Cuchillo y fruta frente a la ventana
Knife and Fruit in Front of the Window
1917
oil on canvas
36 x 36 inches (91.8 x 92.4 cm)
Collection of Museo Dolores Olmedo, Xochimilco, México
Page 27

Naturaleza muerta con planta
Still Life with Plant
1917
oil on canvas
28 x 21 inches (71 x 54 cm)
Collection of Museo Dolores Olmedo, Xochimilco, México
Page 24

Paisaje de midi
Midi Landscape
1918
oil on canvas
31 x 25 inches (79.5 x 63.0 cm)
Collection of Museo Dolores Olmedo, Xochimilco, México

El matemático
The Mathematician
1919
oil on canvas
45½ x 31½ inches (115.5 x 80.5 cm)
Collection of Museo Dolores Olmedo, Xochimilco, México
Page 29

*Día de Flores**
Flower Day
1925
oil on canvas
58 x 47½ inches (147.4 x 120.6 cm)
Collection of the Los Angeles County Museum of Art
Page 63

Mujer moliendo maíz
Woman Grinding Corn
1927
pastel on paper
25 x 19 inches (62.5 x 48.0 cm)
Art Gallery of Ontario. Purchase, 1938
Page 36

Viernes de dolores en Xochimilco
Friday of Sorrows in Xochimilco
1930
lithograph on paper
11 x 16 inches (27.0 x 40.0 cm)
Collection of Museo Dolores Olmedo, Xochimilco, México

Mercado de Tehuantepec
Market of Tehuantepec
1930
lithograph on paper
11 x 16 inches (27.0 x 40.0 cm)
Collection of Museo Dolores Olmedo, Xochimilco, México

Desnudo de Frida Kahlo
Nude of Frida Kahlo
1930
lithograph on paper
17 x 12 inches (44.0 x 30.0 cm)
Collection of Museo Dolores Olmedo, Xochimilco, México

Autorretrato
Self-Portrait
1930
lithograph on paper
16 x 11 inches (40.0 x 28.0 cm)
Collection of Museo Dolores Olmedo, Xochimilco, México

Fiesta de flores: Fiesta de Santa Anita
Flower Festival: Feast of Santa Anita
1931
encaustic on canvas
78 x 64 inches (199.0 x 162.5 cm)
The Museum of Modern Art, New York. Gift of Abby Aldrich Rockefeller, 1936. Digital Image © The Museum of Modern Art/Licensed by SCALA/Art Resource, NY
Page 33

La canoa enflorada
The Flowered Canoe
1931
oil on canvas
79 x 63 inches (200.0 x 160.0 cm)
Collection of Museo Dolores Olmedo, Xochimilco, México
Page 37

Desnudo de Dolores Olmedo
Nude of Dolores Olmedo
1932
lithograph on paper
20 x 16 inches (50.0 x 40.0 cm)
Collection of Museo Dolores Olmedo, Xochimilco, México

El sueño (la noche de los pobres)
Sleep (The Night of the Poor)
1932
lithograph on paper
16 x 12 inches (41.5 x 30.5 cm)
Collection of Museo Dolores Olmedo, Xochimilco, México

El líder campesino Zapata
The Agrarian Leader Zapata
1932
lithograph on paper
16 x 13 inches (41.0 x 33.5 cm)
Collection of Museo Dolores Olmedo, Xochimilco, México
Page 32

El niño del taco
The Boy with the Taco
1932
lithograph on paper
16½ x 12 inches (42.0 x 30.0 cm)
Collection of Museo Dolores Olmedo, Xochimilco, México

Los frutos de la tierra
The Fruits of Labour
1932
lithograph on paper
17 x 12 inches (41.5 x 30.5 cm)
Collection of Museo Dolores Olmedo, Xochimilco, México

La maestra rural
The Rural Schoolteacher
1932
lithograph on paper
12½ x 16½ inches (32 x 42 cm)
Collection of Museo Dolores Olmedo, Xochimilco, México
Page 35

Maternidad mecánica
Mechanical Motherhood
1933
watercolor on paper
18½ x 10 inches (47.0 x 25.0 cm)
Collection of Museo Dolores Olmedo, Xochimilco, México

La familia (Madre e hijos)
The Family (Mother and Children)
1934
oil on canvas
19 x 24 inches (48.0 x 62.0 cm)
Collection of Museo Dolores Olmedo, Xochimilco, México
Page 38

Vendedor de coles
Cabbage Seller
1936
watercolor on paper
15 x 10 inches (38.0 x 26.5 cm)
Collection of Museo Dolores Olmedo, Xochimilco, México
Page 36

Día de los Muertos
Day of the Dead
c. 1936
watercolor with ink and pastel on brown laid paper
19 x 25 inches (48.5 x 62.5 cm)
Art Gallery of Ontario. Gift from the J.S. McLean Collection, by Canada Packers Inc., 1990
Page 39

Cabeza
Head
c. 1936
watercolor on paper
24 x 19 inches (62.0 x 47.5 cm)
Art Gallery of Ontario. Gift from the J.S. McLean Collection, by Canada Packers Inc., 1990
Page 38

Modesta
Modesta
1937
oil on canvas
31½ x 23 inches (80.0 x 59.0 cm)
The Jacques and Natasha Gelman Collection of Mexican Art
Page 59

Mujer con flores
Woman with Flowers
1938
pastel on paper
24 x 18½ inches (62.0 x 47.0 cm)
Collection of Museo Dolores Olmedo, Xochimilco, México

Autorretrato
Self-Portrait
1941
oil on canvas
24 x 16½ inches (60.0 x 42.0 cm)
Collection of Michael Audain and Yoshiko Karasawa
Page 67

Danza al sol
Dance to the Sun
1942
oil on Masonite
77 x 48 inches (196.0 x 122.0 cm)
Collection of Museo Dolores Olmedo, Xochimilco, México

Vendedora de alcatraces
Calla Lily Vendor
1943
oil on Masonite
59 x 47 inches (150.0 x 120.0 cm)
The Jacques and Natasha Gelman Collection of Mexican Art
Page 62

Retrato de Natasha Gelman
Portrait of Natasha Gelman
1943
oil on canvas
45 x 60 inches (115.0 x 153.0 cm)
The Jacques and Natasha Gelman Collection of Mexican Art
Page 72

Girasoles
Sunflowers
1943
oil on canvas
35 x 51 inches (90.0 x 130.0 cm)
The Jacques and Natasha Gelman Collection of Mexican Art
Page 61

El curandero
The Healer
1945
watercolor on paper
18 x 24 inches (46.0 x 60.5 cm)
Collection of Michael Audain and Yoshiko Karasawa

Retrato de Gladys March
Portrait of Gladys March
1946
oil on canvas
30 x 28 inches (76.0 x 71.0 cm)
Collection of Michael Audain and Yoshiko Karasawa
Page 71

Maternidad
Maternity
1954
oil on canvas
36½ x 62 inches (92.5 x 157.0 cm)
Collection of Michael Audain and Yoshiko Karasawa
Page 60

Mujer recogiendo la nieve
Woman Shoveling Snow
1955
watercolor on paper
11 x 15 inches (27 x 38 cm)
Collection of Museo Dolores Olmedo, Xochimilco, México

Niño del Sputnik
Child of Sputnik
1956
oil on canvas
38 x 26 inches (97 x 67 cm)
Collection of Museo Dolores Olmedo, Xochimilco, México

Último refugio de Hitler (Ruinas de la cancillería de Berlín)
The Last Refuge of Hitler (Ruins of the Chancellery of Berlin)
1956
oil and tempera on canvas
41½ x 53 inches (105 x 135 cm)
Private collection, courtesy of Galería Arvil, México

Puesta de sol 2
Sunset 2
1956
oil and tempera on board
15 x 16 inches (39.0 x 41.0 cm)
Collection of Museo Dolores Olmedo, Xochimilco, México
Page 81

Puesta de sol 5
Sunset 5
1956
oil and tempera on board
15 x 16 inches (39.0 x 41.0 cm)
Collection of Museo Dolores Olmedo, Xochimilco, México

Puesta de sol 9
Sunset 9
1956
oil and tempera on board
15 x 16 inches (39.0 x 41.0 cm)
Collection of Museo Dolores Olmedo, Xochimilco, México

Puesta de sol 15
Sunset 15
1956
oil and tempera on board
15 x 16 inches (39.0 x 41.0 cm)
Collection of Museo Dolores Olmedo, Xochimilco, México

Puesta de sol 20
Sunset 20
1956
oil and tempera on board
15 x 16 inches (39.0 x 41.0 cm)
Collection of Museo Dolores Olmedo, Xochimilco, México
Page 81

La hamaca
The Hammock
1956
oil and tempera on canvas
41 x 80 inches (104.0 x 202.0 cm)
Collection of Museo Dolores Olmedo, Xochimilco, México
Page 80

Las sandias
The Watermelons
1957
oil on canvas
27 x 36 inches (68.0 x 92.0 cm)
Collection of Museo Dolores Olmedo, Xochimilco, México

Photographs in Chronological Order*

Anonymous
Frida Kahlo, 2 Years Old
1909–1910
gelatin silver print
Courtesy of Throckmorton Fine Arts, Inc., New York

Edward Weston
born Highland Park, Illinois, United States, 1886; died Big Sur, California, United States, 1958
Diego Rivera
1924
gelatin silver print
The Museum of Modern Art, New York. Gift of David H. McAlpin, 1956

Tina Modotti
born Udine, Italy, 1896; died Mexico City, Mexico, 1942
Untitled (Rivera Speaking)
c. 1925
gelatin silver print; printed 1976 by Richard Benson
The Museum of Modern Art, New York. Courtesy of Isabel Carbajal Bolandi

Tina Modotti
Flagellation of Christ
c. 1925–1927
gelatin silver print
Collection: Ann and Harry Malcolmson

Tina Modotti
Worker Reading El Machete
1927
gelatin silver print
Collection: Ann and Harry Malcolmson
Page 31

*Selection of photographs may vary for each exhibition

Tina Modotti
Hands of a Washerwoman
c. 1927–1928
platinum print
Collection: Ann and Harry Malcolmson

Tina Modotti
Marionette: René d'Harnoncourt
1929
gelatin silver print
Private collection

Tina Modotti
Marionette and Bird
1929
gelatin silver print
Collection, Patricia Regan

Victor Reyes
Diego Rivera and his Bride, Coyoacán, Mexico
1929
vintage gelatin silver print
Courtesy of Throckmorton Fine Arts, Inc., New York

Agustín Jiménez
born Mexico City, Mexico, 1901; died Mexico, 1974
Diego Rivera
c. 1930s
vintage gelatin silver print
Courtesy of Throckmorton Fine Arts, Inc., New York

Peter A. Juley & Son
Diego Rivera and Frida Kahlo in the Studio of Sculptor Ralph Stackpole, Montgomery Street, San Francisco, CA
1931
gelatin silver print
Courtesy of Throckmorton Fine Arts, Inc., New York

Peter A. Juley & Son
Diego Rivera before his Painting The Agrarian Leader Zapata
1931
photograph
The Museum of Modern Art, New York; Photographic Archive, Exhibition Albums 14.2. The Museum of Modern Art Archives, New York

Peter A. Juley & Son
Diego Rivera Painting Liberation of the Peon
1931
photograph
The Museum of Modern Art, New York. Photographic Archive, Exhibition Albums 14.1. The Museum of Modern Art Archives, New York

Peter A. Juley & Son
Frida Kahlo in the Studio of Sculptor Ralph Stackpole, Montgomery Street, San Francisco, CA
1931
gelatin silver print
Courtesy of Throckmorton Fine Arts, Inc., New York

Imogen Cunningham
born Portland, Oregon, United States, 1883; died San Francisco, California, United States, 1976
Frida Kahlo Rivera
1931
gelatin silver print
High Museum of Art. Purchase, with funds from a Friend of the Museum

Manuel Álvarez Bravo
born and died Mexico City, Mexico, 1902–2002
Portrait of Diego Rivera
1930–1940
gelatin silver print; printed later
Courtesy of Throckmorton Fine Arts, Inc., New York

Manuel Álvarez Bravo
Portrait: Lola Bravo
1932
vintage silver gelatin print
Collection: Ann and Harry Malcolmson

Acme Photo
Diego and Frida in New York City
1933
vintage gelatin silver print
Courtesy of Throckmorton Fine Arts, Inc., New York

Anonymous
Diego Rivera – Painter Dropped by Rockefellers
c. 1933
vintage gelatin silver print
Courtesy of Throckmorton Fine Arts, Inc., New York

Anonymous
Diego Rivera and Frida Kahlo, Detroit
c. 1933
vintage gelatin silver print
Courtesy of Throckmorton Fine Arts, Inc., New York
Page 8

Martin Munkácsi
born Kolozsvár, Hungary, 1896; died New York City, New York, United States, 1963
Frida and Diego
1934
vintage gelatin silver print
Courtesy of Throckmorton Fine Arts, Inc., New York

Anonymous
Frida Kahlo and Diego Rivera in Diego's Studio
1934
vintage gelatin silver print
Courtesy of Throckmorton Fine Arts, Inc., New York

Guillermo Davila
born 1898; died 1990
Frida Kahlo, Outside Diego Rivera's Studio, Mexico
c. 1935
gelatin silver print
Courtesy of Throckmorton Fine Arts, Inc., New York

Nickolas Muray
born Szeged, Hungary, 1892; died New York City, New York, United States, 1965
Frida and Diego (with gas mask kissing), Coyoacán
1938
giclée print
Courtesy and © Nickolas Muray Photo Archives

Nickolas Muray
Frida Kahlo with Olmeca Figurine, Coyoacán
1939
carbon print
Courtesy and © Nickolas Muray Photo Archives

Nickolas Muray
Frida on White Bench, New York
1939
giclée print
Courtesy and © Nickolas Muray Photo Archives

Nickolas Muray
Frida Painting The Two Fridas, *Coyoacán*
1939
gelatin silver print
Courtesy and © Nickolas Muray Photo Archives
Page 4

Nickolas Muray
Frida with Blue Satin Blouse, New York
1939
carbon print
Courtesy and © Nickolas Muray Photo Archives

Nickolas Muray
Frida with Granizo, Coyoacán
1939
gelatin silver print
Courtesy and © Nickolas Muray Photo Archives

Nickolas Muray
Frida with Magenta Rebozo, New York
1939
giclée print
Courtesy and © Nickolas Muray Photo Archives

Nickolas Muray
Frida with Magenta Rebozo (The Breton Portrait), New York
1939
carbon print
Courtesy and © Nickolas Muray Photo Archives

Nickolas Muray
Frida (with Picasso earrings), Coyoacán
1939
carbon print
Courtesy and © Nickolas Muray Photo Archives

Anonymous
Frida and Diego Kissing after Second Marriage
1940
gelatin silver print
Courtesy of Throckmorton Fine Arts, Inc., New York

Bernard Silberstein
born Illinois, United States, 1905; died Cincinnati, Ohio, United States, 1999
Frida Kahlo in her Bedroom
1940
sepia-toned gelatin silver print; printed later
Courtesy of Throckmorton Fine Arts, Inc., New York

Bernard Silberstein
Frida Kahlo Painting The Wounded Table, *Mexico*
1940
gelatin silver print; printed later
Courtesy of Throckmorton Fine Arts, Inc., New York

Bernard Silberstein
Frida Paints Self-Portrait while Diego Watches
c. 1940
sepia-toned gelatin silver print; printed later
Courtesy of Throckmorton Fine Arts, Inc., New York
Page 10

Bernard Silberstein
Frida with Pottery Objects and Judas Figure
c. 1940
gelatin silver print
Courtesy of Throckmorton Fine Arts, Inc., New York

Nickolas Muray
Blanche Hays, Frida Kahlo, Nickolas Muray, Emmy Lou Packard, Arija Muray and Diego Rivera Seated
c. 1940
gelatin silver print
Art Gallery of Ontario. Gift of Kate Hays, 2012

Nickolas Muray
Frida and Diego with Hat, San Angel
1941
gelatin silver print
Courtesy and © Nickolas Muray Photo Archives

Nickolas Muray
Frida in the Dining Area, Coyoacán
1941
giclée print
Courtesy and © Nickolas Muray Photo Archives

Nickolas Muray
Frida Painting Me and My Parrots *(with Nick in studio), Coyoacán*
1941
gelatin silver print
Courtesy and © Nickolas Muray Photo Archives

Emmy Lou Packard
born Imperial Valley, California, United States, 1914; died San Francisco, California, United States, 1998
Diego Rivera and Frida Kahlo
1941
platinum print
Emmy Lou Packard papers, Archives of American Art, Smithsonian Institution
Page 84

Florence Arquin
born and died New York City, New York, United States, 1900–1974
Frida Kahlo, Mexico
c. 1941
gelatin silver print
Courtesy of Throckmorton Fine Arts, Inc., New York

Fritz Henle
born Dortmund, Germany, 1909; died Saint Croix, U.S. Virgin Islands, 1993
Frida in her Studio
c. 1943
vintage gelatin silver print
Courtesy of Throckmorton Fine Arts, Inc., New York

Anonymous
Portrait of André Breton in Mexico
c. 1943
gelatin silver print
Collection of FEMSA

Lola Álvarez Bravo
born Jalisco, Mexico, 1907; died Mexico City, Mexico, 1993
Frida Kahlo
1944
gelatin silver print
Courtesy of Throckmorton Fine Arts, Inc., New York

Lola Álvarez Bravo
Frida Kahlo Seated with Dogs
1944
gelatin silver print
Courtesy of Throckmorton Fine Arts, Inc., New York

Lola Álvarez Bravo
Frida Kahlo with Dogs and Idol
1944
gelatin silver print
Courtesy of Throckmorton Fine Arts, Inc., New York

Lola Álvarez Bravo
Frida Looking into a Mirror
c. 1944
gelatin silver print
Courtesy of Throckmorton Fine Arts, Inc., New York

Nickolas Muray
Frida (on the roof), New York
1946
carbon print
Courtesy and © Nickolas Muray Photo Archives

Anonymous
Frida and Diego at a Rally
1940s
gelatin silver print
Courtesy of Throckmorton Fine Arts, Inc., New York
Page 14

Lola Álvarez Bravo
Frida Seated in Hospital Room with Photographs
c. 1940s
gelatin silver print; printed in 1990
Courtesy of Throckmorton Fine Arts, Inc., New York

Juan Guzmán (Hans Gutmann Guster)
born Cologne, Germany, 1911; died Mexico, 1982
Frida with Two Birds
c. late 1940s
platinum print
Courtesy of Throckmorton Fine Arts, Inc., New York

Héctor García
born and died Mexico City, Mexico, 1923–2012
Frida with Itzcuintli Dog
1949
vintage gelatin silver print
Courtesy of Throckmorton Fine Arts, Inc., New York

Lola Álvarez Bravo
Frida Kahlo
1950
gelatin silver print
Courtesy of Throckmorton Fine Arts, Inc., New York

Lola Álvarez Bravo
Frida Kahlo (lying on bed)
1950
gelatin silver print
Courtesy of Throckmorton Fine Arts, Inc., New York

Lola Álvarez Bravo
Frida Kahlo (leaning against bedpost)
1950
gelatin silver print
Courtesy of Throckmorton Fine Arts, Inc., New York

Lola Álvarez Bravo
Frida Kahlo (looking at mirror)
1950
gelatin silver print
Courtesy of Throckmorton Fine Arts, Inc., New York

Bernice Kolko
born Grayevo, Poland, 1905; died Mexico City, Mexico, 1970
Frida Kahlo
c. 1950–1954
gelatin silver print
High Museum of Art, Atlanta. Purchase, 1977

Juan Guzmán (Hans Gutmann Guster)
Untitled – Frida Posing for Diego Rivera's Mural The Nightmare of War and the Dream of Peace *in the Palacio de Bellas Artes, Mexico*
1952
vintage gelatin silver print
Colección Juan Guzmán, Archivo Fotográfico del Instituto de Investigaciones Estéticas, UNAM
Page 86

Lola Álvarez Bravo
Frida Kahlo Funeral Bed
1954
gelatin silver print mounted on board
Courtesy of Throckmorton Fine Arts, Inc., New York

Lola Álvarez Bravo
Frida Kahlo on her Deathbed
1954
vintage gelatin silver print
Courtesy of Throckmorton Fine Arts, Inc., New York

Bernice Kolko
Funeral of Frida Kahlo with Diego
1954
gelatin silver print
High Museum of Art, Atlanta. Purchase, 1977

Héctor García
Frida Kahlo in Coffin with Diego Rivera at Funeral
1954
vintage gelatin silver print, glossy
Courtesy of Throckmorton Fine Arts, Inc., New York
Page 85

Héctor García
Portrait of Diego Rivera in Studio
1956
gelatin silver print
High Museum of Art, Atlanta. Purchase, 1989

G.Y. Massart
Diego Rivera Deathbed
1957
gelatin silver print
Courtesy of Throckmorton Fine Arts, Inc., New York

G.Y. Massart
Diego Rivera's Funeral
1957
gelatin silver print
Courtesy of Throckmorton Fine Arts, Inc., New York
Page 85

Diego Rivera Frescoes at the Ministry of Education, Mexico City

Asemblea
Assembly
1923–1924
Courtyard of Festivities/First Level
Page 30

La maestra rural
The Rural Schoolteacher
1923–1924
Courtyard of Work/First Level
Page 34

El Arsenal
The Arsenal
1928–1929
Courtyard of Festivities/Third Level
from the mural cycle *Ballad of the Proletarian Revolution/Ballad of the Agrarian Revolution*
Page 40

All mural reproductions are courtesy of Schalkwijk/Art Resource, NY & Secretaria de Educación Pública, Mexico City, D.F., Mexico. © Artists Rights Society (ARS), New York

Catalogue Images Not Exhibited at the AGO or the High

Paul A. Juley
born 1867; died 1937
Frida Kahlo and Diego Rivera
1931
Chester Dale papers, Archives of American Art, Smithsonian Institution
Page 1

Anonymous
Diego Rivera in Paris (at age 32)
1919
© Banco de México Diego Rivera & Frida Kahlo Museums Trust, Mexico, D.F./Agustin Estrada
Page 2

Guillermo Kahlo
born Pforzheim, Germany, 1871; died Mexico City, Mexico, 1941
Frida Kahlo in Coyoacán (at age 11)
1919
© Banco de México Diego Rivera & Frida Kahlo Museums Trust, Mexico, D.F./Agustin Estrada
Page 3

Victor De Palma
Diego Rivera Working on a Mural with Plate-shaped Palette in Hand
1944
© Pix Inc. Time Life Pictures/Getty Images
Page 5

Guillermo Zamora
born 1913; died 2002
Diego and Frida in the Casa Azul
c. 1952
© Banco de México Diego Rivera & Frida Kahlo Museums Trust, Mexico, D.F./Agustin Estrada
Page 21

Anonymous
Frida Kahlo and Diego Rivera
c. 1933
Albert Kahn papers, Archives of American Art, Smithsonian Institution
Page 41

Lucienne Bloch
born Geneva, Switzerland, 1909; died Gualala, California, United States, 1999
Frida in Front of the Unfinished Unity Panel, New Workers School, New York City
1933
© Estate of Lucienne Bloch (www.LucienneBloch.com)
Page 43

Anonymous
Kahlo's mother Matilde Calderón (circled), age 7, with her Oaxacan family
1890
© Banco de México Diego Rivera & Frida Kahlo Museums Trust, Mexico, D.F./Agustin Estrada
Page 48

Anonymous
André Breton, Diego Rivera, Leon Trotsky, and Jacqueline Lamba in Mexico
1938
Courtesy of Snark/Art Resource, NY. © Artists Rights Society (ARS), New York
Page 64

Juan Guzmán (Hans Gutmann Guster)
Frida in Hospital Painting her Cast
1940s
gelatin silver print
Colección Juan Guzmán, Archivo Fotográfico del Instituto de Investigaciones Estéticas, UNAM
Page 76

Pre-Columbian Objects in the AGO Exhibition

Waterbearer Figure
Origin/Period: Zapotec
Proto-Classic (100 BC–250 AD)
On loan from the Royal Ontario Museum, Toronto

Crouching Jaguar Sculpture
Origin/Period: Zapotec
Classic (250–900 AD)
On loan from the Royal Ontario Museum, Toronto

Flat Female Figure
Origin/Period: Colima
Proto-Classic (100 BC–250 AD)
On loan from the Royal Ontario Museum, Toronto. The Mr. & Mrs. Samuel J. Zacks Collection

Jade Mask
Origin/Period: Olmec
Pre-Classic (900–600 BC)
On loan from the Royal Ontario Museum, Toronto. Gift of Mrs. Irene Emerson

Male Figure
Origin/Period: Nayarit
Proto-Classic (100 BC–250 AD)
On loan from the Royal Ontario Museum, Toronto. A gift in memory of Jean Nathanson Shawn

Female Figure
Origin/Period: Nayarit
Proto-Classic (100 BC–250 AD)
On loan from the Royal Ontario Museum, Toronto. A gift in memory of Jean Nathanson Shawn

Pot-bellied Dog Figurine
Origin/Period: Colima
Proto-Classic (100 BC–250 AD)
On loan from the Royal Ontario Museum, Toronto. Gift of David Robertson

Nursing Figure
Origin/Period: Nayarit
Proto-Classic (100 BC–250 AD)
On loan from the Royal Ontario Museum, Toronto. Gift of David Robertson

ACKNOWLEDGMENTS

A collaboration of this scale and ambition involves contributions from every department of each institution. Our talented and hard-working staffs deserve our gratitude. At the High, a core team has been working on this collaboration since the beginning: David Brenneman, Director of Collections and Exhibitions and Frances B. Bunzl Family Curator of European Art; Philip Verre, Chief Operating Officer; and Jody Cohen, Senior Manager of Special Initiatives, have overseen the development and implementation of this exhibition. At the Art Gallery of Ontario, the exhibition was championed by Matthew Teitelbaum, Michael and Sonja Koerner Director & CEO, and Elizabeth Smith, Executive Director of Curatorial Affairs, and led by Iain Hoadley, Interim Head, Exhibition Operations and Senior Project Manager.

The multifaceted nature of such an exhibition relies on the keen organizational skills and judgment of a team of colleagues. At the High, we deeply appreciate the efforts of Rhonda Matheison, Chief Financial Officer; Amy Simon, Manager of Exhibitions; Laurie Kind, Images and Rights Coordinator; Elizabeth Riccardi, Assistant to the Director of Collections and Exhibitions; Toni Pentecouteau, Executive Assistant to the Director; and Leslie Petsoff, Assistant to the Chief Operating Officer. Our registration and installation departments managed the considerable task of mobilizing more than 100 works at the High smoothly and efficiently. Frances Francis, Senior Registrar; Rebecca Parker, Associate Registrar; and Jeremy Underwood, Coordinator for Collections and Exhibitions, oversaw transport and loans. Brian Kelly, Chief Preparator; Gene Clifton, Senior Preparator, Fabrication; and Cayse Cheatham, Edward Hill, and Caroline Prinzivalli, Preparators, all made sure that the works were safely received and beautifully installed in Atlanta, as did Kevin Streiter, Manager of Facilities and Logistics, and Al Holland, Chief of Security. The AGO is equally grateful to our exhibition services team who have played key roles throughout multiple phases of this endeavor, including George Bartosik, Manager, Exhibition Services; Akira Yoshikawa, Collections Care Specialist, Access and Processing Coordinator; Tim Hardacre, Collections Care Specialist, Storage

Coordinator; Curtis Strilchuk, Registrar, Exhibitions; Alison Beckett, Loans Coordinator; Dale Mahar, Traffic Coordinator; Brian Groombridge, Installation Coordinator; Charles Kettle, Production Coordinator, Exhibition Services; and Debbie Johnson, Curatorial Administrative Assistant, Modern and Contemporary Art.

For helping to relay this rich material to our visitors, educators at both museums deserve our thanks: at the High, Julia Forbes, Shannon Landing Amos Head of Museum Interpretation; Virginia Shearer, Associate Chair of Public Programs; Erin Dougherty, Manager of Family Programs and New Audience Initiatives; Lisa Hooten, Head of School Programs; and Nicole Cromartie, Coordinator of Museum Interpretation. At the AGO, the contributions of David Wistow, Interpretive Planner, and Keri Ryan, Manager, Interpretation and Visitor Research, have been vital in this regard.

The High extends its appreciation to the development and finance teams who have secured the funding and sponsorships that make such a large-scale endeavor possible: Kimberly Watson, Director of Museum Advancement, and Ruth Richardson, Manager of Individual Support. The AGO acknowledges Lisa Landreth, Associate Director, Individual Giving, and Tessa Bulham, Associate Director, Partnerships.

Our communications teams have conveyed this exhibition's complex subject matter to the press and the public with clarity and style. At the High, we are grateful to Jennifer Bahus, Senior Manager of Advertising and Promotions, and Kristen Heflin, Public Relations Manager. For building new museum memberships around this project, we also thank Catherine Fink, Senior Manager of Membership and Guest Relations; Jennifer McNally, Member and Guest Relations Manager; and Jodi O'Gara, Manager of Group Sales. The AGO wishes to acknowledge Steve Rayment, Director of Marketing, Design & Publicity; Andrea Seaborn, Manager of Marketing; Patricia Mewdell, Marketing Coordinator; Caitlin Coull, Manager of Communications; Meagan Campbell, Internet and Social Media Content Coordinator; and Andrea-Jo Wilson, News Officer.

The High has been fortunate to rely on Jim Waters, Exhibition Designer, for his imaginative solutions in presenting objects. Contributing extensively to the High project's overall look were Angela Jaeger, Senior Manager of Creative Services, and Ewan Green, Graphic Designer, as well as editors Rachel Bohan and Heather Medlock. The AGO is fortunate to have had the talented Evelina Petrauskas, 2-D Graphic Designer, and Flavio Trevisan, 3-D Exhibition Designer, on hand to bring this unique exhibition to fruition, aided by the tireless efforts of Malene Hjorngaard, Production Coordinator. The publication was skillfully executed by Jim Shedden, Head of Digital Content and Publishing, whose dedicated team included Sean Weaver, Photographer & Coordinator, Image Resources; Syvalya Elchen, Image Rights & Reproductions Coordinator; Daniel Naccarato, Editor, Digital Content & Publications; as well as Linda Gustafson at Counterpunch, who designed this remarkable book with flair and aplomb.

The Art Gallery of Ontario is partially funded by the Ontario Ministry of Culture. Additional operating support is received from the Volunteers of the Art Gallery of Ontario, City of Toronto, the Department of Canadian Heritage, and the Canada Council for the Arts.

This catalogue is published in conjunction with the exhibition:
Frida & Diego: Passion, Politics and Painting
Art Gallery of Ontario
October 20, 2012–January 20, 2013

Frida & Diego: Passion, Politics, and Painting
High Museum of Art, Atlanta
February 16–May 12, 2013

Library and Archives Canada Cataloguing in Publication

Tuer, Dot
Frida & Diego : passion, politics and painting / Dot Tuer and Elliott King.

Published on the occasion of an exhibition held at the Art Gallery of Ontario, October 20, 2012–January 20, 2013.
Includes bibliographical references.
ISBN 978-1-894243-71-1

1. Kahlo, Frida – Exhibitions. 2. Rivera, Diego, 1886–1957 – Exhibitions. 3. Painting, Mexican – Exhibitions. 4. Painting, Modern – 20th century – Exhibitions. 5. Art – Political aspects – Exhibitions. I. Kahlo, Frida II. Rivera, Diego, 1886–1957
III. King, Elliott H. IV. Art Gallery of Ontario
V. Title. VI. Title: Frida and Diego.

ND259.K33A4 2012 759.972 C2012-904566-7

Editing/proofreading: Daniel Naccarato
Graphic designer: Linda Gustafson/Counterpunch Inc.
AGO photography: Sean Weaver
Printed and bound in Canada by Type A Print Inc.

Art Gallery of Ontario
317 Dundas Street West
Toronto, Ontario, Canada M5T 1G4
www.ago.net

High Museum of Art
1280 Peachtree Street, N.E.
Atlanta, Georgia 30309
www.high.org

Distribution:
D.A.P./Distributed Art Publishers, Inc.
155 6th Avenue, 2nd floor
New York, NY 10013
1-212-627-1999
www.artbook.com